HABAKKUK
AND
ZEPHANIAH

HABAKKUK
AND
ZEPHANIAH

by
CYRIL J. BARBER

MOODY PRESS
CHICAGO

© 1985 by
THE MOODY BIBLE INSTITUTE
OF CHICAGO

Unless otherwise noted, all quotations and/or paraphrases of Scripture
in this book are the author's.

Selected references from the *New American Standard Bible,* © 1960,
1962, 1963, 1968, 1971, 1972, 1973, 1975, and 1977 by the Lockman Foundation
are used by permission.

Library of Congress Cataloging in Publication Data

Barber, Cyril J.
  Habakkuk and Zephaniah.

  Bibliography: p. 127
  1. Bible. O.T. Habakkuk—Commentaries.
2. Bible. O.T. Zephaniah—Commentaries. I. Title.
BS1635.3.B37 1985   224'.9507   85-2960
ISBN 0-8024-2069-9 (pbk.)

1 2 3 4 5 6 7 Printing/EP/Year 90 89 88 87 86 85

Printed in the United States of America

For . . .
    SHARALEE ASPENLEITER
    Coauthor, Colleague, Friend.
    In sincere appreciation and
    affection.

CONTENTS

PREFACE

When a well-worn Bible is allowed to fall open at random, the possibility of its opening at the book of Psalms or the gospel of John or one of the epistles is good. Even among zealous Bible students, the books of Habakkuk and Zephaniah are seldom read. One is tempted with the thought that if they were somehow surreptitiously removed from the Bible, they would not be missed.

But why have these books been so neglected?

In Habakkuk, we encounter difficulties in translation (particularly in chap. 3) that are perplexing and hard to unravel. The late George Adam Smith, for many years principal of the University of Aberdeen, Scotland, stated in his exposition of the Minor Prophets, "The Book of Zephaniah is one of the most difficult in the prophetic canon." Without doubt, the interpretive difficulties surrounding the writings of this Old Testament prophet have turned many away.

That which follows in the pages of this book is not intended for scholars. My aim in expounding these prophetic writings has been to explain the central purpose of each book. In doing so, I have attempted to adhere to a consistent literal hermeneutic. Those who have attempted to grapple with the diversity of literary forms found in these writings know better than to be dogmatic. What I have presented, therefore, I hope will stimulate further inquiry into these long-neglected portions of God's Word.

I want to say a very special word of thanks to Philip Rawley, former textbook editor, Moody Press, for inviting me to contribute to the Everyman's Bible Commentary series. In addition, I would like to express my gratitude to my secretary, Mrs. Michael (Marilyn) Moore, and my research

assistant, Mrs. Steve (Janet) McCracken, without whose inde-
fatigable efforts this manuscript would not have been ready
on time.

HABAKKUK

1

INTRODUCTION TO HABAKKUK

The book of Habakkuk was written to people facing change—imminent change—in their political, economic, social, and religious lives. As such, it has a direct bearing upon contemporary society.

In his book *Managing in Turbulent Times,* Peter Drucker points an unerring finger at Western civilization and warns of the "irregular, non-linear, erratic" times facing modern society. He describes the twenty-five years following World War II and shows how a high degree of continuity and productivity characterized the West, as well as the emerging Third World countries. Now, however, an era of rapid change has begun that calls for new strategies—strategies that can anticipate the changes that surely will come.

"A time of turbulence" is a "dangerous time," he writes.

> Its greatest danger is a temptation to deny reality. The new realities fit neither the assumption of the Left nor those of the Right. . . . The greatest and most dangerous turbulence today results from the collision between the delusions of the decisionmakers . . . and the realities [facing us at the present time].[1]

In that respect, there is a remarkable correlation between the situation today and the one that faced Judah in the days of Habakkuk. The peace that had accompanied the reign of Josiah (640-609 B.C.) had allowed the people to enjoy a greater degree of prosperity than had been possible for many years. In a real sense they thought the new era would last indefinitely. The realities that faced them, however, could not have been an-

1. P. Drucker, *Managing in Turbulent Times* (New York: Harper and Row, 1980), pp. 4-5.

ticipated by either the political liberals or the religiously-minded conservatives.

The power of Assyria had collapsed. Political supremacy belonged to Egypt. Strong political ties, however, had been established with the emerging kingdom of Babylon. Because she was a vassal of Egypt and a friend of Babylon, it seemed as if nothing could threaten the progress of Judah's prosperity.

The nation owed its prosperity to God's favoring of one man, Josiah (2 Kings 22:1, 12-17). Josiah had led the nation in several notable reforms. Although those reforms touched only the outward observances of the people, God said He would honor Josiah for his faithfulness (2 Kings 22:18-20).[2]

The leaders of the people ignored the spiritual reasons for their material prosperity and thought God's favor could be enjoyed without interruption. J. Gresham Machen once remarked, "America is running on the momentum of a Godly ancestry. When that momentum goes, God help America!" The same could be said of Judah in Habakkuk's day. It was not long before greed and avarice became prevalent. The rich exploited the poor. "Justice" favored the wealthy. Those who were God-fearing found themselves oppressed by an ever-increasing number whose desire for power led them to secure, by one means or another, those positions that met their personal (and often pathological) needs.

It was amid such conditions that God revealed His will to Habakkuk. Turbulent times lay ahead for the Lord's people. The message Habakkuk was told to proclaim was one that would please neither the Left nor the Right. The delusions of the decision makers were to be dashed to pieces before the harsh reality of God's sovereign justice.

I. AUTHORSHIP AND DATE

The book of Habakkuk takes its name from its author. Today practically nothing is known of Habakkuk, though much conjecture has arisen about him. It is thought by some that his

2. L. Wood, *A Survey of Israel's History* (Grand Rapids: Zondervan, 1970), pp. 366-73.

name came from the Hebrew word *habhak*, "to embrace" or "the embraced." Davidson has suggested that his name was "really an abstract noun used in the concrete sense of an object that is embraced and so means 'darling.' "[3] Luther believed that his name meant "the heartner," and stated that the prophet was "one who takes another to his heart and [into] his arms, as one soothes a poor weeping child, telling it to be quiet."[4]

Little information can be gleaned about Habakkuk from either the Septuagint or the Vulgate translations.

Several clues as to the prophet's identity are to be found in his record of God's revelation. Those clues are not numerous. Habakkuk did not follow the usual policy of dating his prophecy in the reign of a king (cf. Zeph. 1:1), but he did state that he was a "prophet" (lit. "the prophet"). Inasmuch as the term denoted an official position (cf. Nah. 1:1), he must be accorded a place with the other men and women in the Old Testament who spoke forth the word of the Lord. The reference in 2:2 supports that identity and tacitly intimates that those in the prophet's time who read what he had written would respond to the message communicated to them.

A further clue as to Habakkuk's identity may be gleaned from references in 3:1 and 3:19*d*. The former is a musical ascription, "Shigionoth," and the latter is a subscription at the end of the book, "For the choir director, on my stringed instruments" (NASB). The references support one another and may intimate that Habakkuk was a Levite and a singer in the Temple.

It is interesting to note the extent to which legend has grown up around the person of Habakkuk. In past times some rabbis have imagined that there was a connection between his name and the words the prophet Elisha had spoken to the Shunammite woman to assure her that she would "embrace a son" (2 Kings 4:16, NASB). Those rabbis have believed that Habakkuk

---

3. A. B. Davidson, *The Books of Nahum, Habakkuk and Zephaniah,* Cambridge Bible for Schools and Colleges (Cambridge: Cambridge U., 1905), p. 45.
4. M. Luther, *Lectures on the Minor Prophets,* vol. 19 of *Luther's Works,* ed. H. C. Oswald (St. Louis: Concordia, 1974), 2:156.

was the woman's son. Others have seen a link between Habakkuk's vigil of 2:2 and a vigil described in Isaiah 21:6. Those
who adhere to that theory are quick to identify the prophet
with the watchman appointed to stand upon the walls of
Jerusalem and watch for the fall of Babylon.

When consideration is given to extra-biblical traditions, a
reference to a man named Habakkuk can be found in the
apocryphal book of "Daniel, Bel, and the Snake" (Bel, 33ff.),
better known as "Bel and the Dragon." In that account,
Habakkuk, while in Judea, made a stew and was carrying it out
to the reapers who were in the field. An angel of the Lord was
supposed to have appeared to him and said, "Habakkuk, carry
the meal you have with you to Babylon, for Daniel, who is in
the lion-pit." To this Habakkuk responded, "My lord, I have
never been to Babylon. I do not know where the lion-pit is."
Then the angel, according to the theory, lifted the prophet up
into the air by the hairs of his head and, with the blast of the
breath of his mouth, swept him away to Babylon where he
miraculously came down above the pit where Daniel was im-
prisoned. Such a view strains our credulity and is unworthy of
serious attention.

The ministry of the prophet was intimately connected with
the date of his prophecy, and, while the traditional dating of
the book (around 605 B.C.) has been accepted by the majority
of liberal and conservative scholars, closer examination of the
evidence supports a date a few years earlier.

Although Pusey prefers to date Habakkuk's oracle in the
reign of Manasseh (some time before 642 B.C.), such an early
date is too soon for the Babylonians to have become well
known for the atrocities described in chapters 1 and 2.[5]

At the other end of the continuum is B. Duhm, who is
followed by several notable scholars, including C. C. Torrey.
By changing the word "Chaldean" (*Kasdîm*) in Habakkuk 1:6
to "Cypriot' or "Greek" (*Kittîm*), Duhm conjectures that
Habakkuk's prophecy could not be dated much before 331 B.C.
(or between the battles of Issus and Arbela). It should be

5. E. B. Pusey, *The Minor Prophets* (Grand Rapids: Baker, 1953), 2:169-72.

pointed out, however, that there is absolutely no warrant for making such a change, and Duhm's theory has not been widely accepted.[6]

In arriving at a more realistic date of Habakkuk's prophecy, it needs to be borne in mind that the Neo-Babylonian empire did not arise to a position of any significance in the ancient Near East until around 625 B.C. That was in the reign of King Josiah (640-609 B.C.), while Assyria was still the leading nation at the time. Unger is inclined to date Habakkuk's prophecy soon after the fall of Nineveh in 612 B.C., but there are those who believe that a date a year or two before Nineveh's demise is preferable. If that view is correct, it would make what God revealed to Habakkuk about the Chaldeans even more surprising (cf. 1:5).

A large number of conservative Bible scholars, however, prefer to date Habakkuk's oracle during the reign of Jehoiakim (609-598 B.C.; 2 Kings 24:1-5; 2 Chron. 36:4-8).[7] They do so on the grounds that the events described in 1:2-4 could only have taken place after Josiah was slain at Megiddo (2 Chron. 35:20-27). Josiah was succeeded by Jehoahaz (2 Kings 23:31-33), who reigned for only three months before being deposed by Pharaoh-Neco and deported to Egypt. Pharaoh-Neco placed Eliakim, one of Josiah's sons, on the throne and changed his name to Jehoiakim (2 Kings 23:34). It was Jehoiakim who saw the three Babylonian invasions that took place between 605 and 598 B.C.

The reasons advanced for dating Habakkuk's prophecy in the time of Jehoiakim are based on passages in the book of Jeremiah that describe essentially the same conditions as those found in 1:2-4 (cf. Jer. 11:10ff.; 14:7, 10-12, 20; 20:8). Although a date toward the end of Josiah's reign is possible, God's words in 2:2-3 intimate an event shortly before 605 B.C., when Nebuchadnezzar took Jerusalem and carried off certain

6. B. Duhm, *Das Buch Habakkuk* (Tübingen: J. C. B. Mohr, 1906), p. 20.
7. C. L. Feinberg, *The Minor Prophets* (Chicago: Moody, 1976), p. 205; F. E. Gaebelein, *Four Minor Prophets* (Chicago: Moody, 1970), pp. 145-46; R. K. Harrison, *Introduction to the Old Testament* (Grand Rapids: Eerdmans, 1969), pp. 932-37.

of the people (cf. Dan. 1:1). A date around 608-606 B.C. thus seems highly likely.

II. The Unity of the Book

Some biblical scholars have claimed that Habakkuk could not have written the three chapters ascribed to him (and there are those who believe he wrote only 1:5-10 and 14-17). Such a negative approach to the text yields nothing of value, and there are relatively few who deny Habakkuk's authorship. With the discovery of the Dead Sea Scrolls, it was found that the "Habakkuk Commentary" ended at chapter 2. This added fuel to the fire of those who had claimed that Habakkuk could not have written chapter 3. Chapter 3, however, did not suit the Essene commentators' hermeneutical purpose, and so the omission of chapter 3 from their copy of the book can be accounted for quite easily. The poem that makes up chapter 3 is a triumphal climax to the problem posed in the first two chapters. When studied in light of the context of the prophet's faith (2:4), it is seen to reach its zenith in a joyful shout of confidence in the LORD as the God of Habakkuk's salvation (3:18).

The criticisms advanced against the literary unity of the book have all been answered, and W. F. Albright has silenced many criticisms by stating that, in his opinion, chapter 3 is an integral part of Habakkuk's prophecy.[8] Habakkuk showed that God controls the destinies of men and peoples, and is Himself governed by discernable principles of morality and righteousness. In the book, therefore, God's justice was vindicated, and an accurate view of history was made possible by demonstrating God's involvement in human affairs.

III. The Theme of the Book

Habakkuk centered his prophecy on a question that all of God's people have asked at one time or another: Why do the

8. W. F. Albright, "The Psalm of Habakkuk," in *Studies of the Old Testament Prophecy Presented to T. H. Robinson,* ed. H. H. Rowley (Edinburgh: T. and T. Clark, 1950), pp. 2, 9.

wicked flourish while the godly are oppressed?[9] In a real sense, therefore, the book of Habakkuk constitutes a theodicy, or a defense of God's goodness and omnipotence in view of evil. It also illustrates the ways in which the just may live by their faith. That concept, as Gaebelein points out, constitutes one of the most dynamic ideas in world history.[10]

In developing his theme, Habakkuk structured his material around two dialogues, with a concluding psalm of praise.

In the first dialogue (1:1-11), the prophet voiced his complaint over the sins of God's people and God's apparent indifference (1:1-4). He described graphically and yet concisely the unscrupulous conduct of those who oppressed the godly. He also described the violence that had come to characterize Judean society. In the midst of that description of lawlessness, Habakkuk asked why God had caused him to look upon such affliction and yet seemed to be indifferent to his prayers.

In answer to His servant's complaint (1:5-11), God showed Habakkuk that He was not indifferent to the plight of His people. In fact, He had been at work raising up the Chaldeans, whom He would use to chasten His people. Their conquest was soon to begin (605 B.C.).

That response to his prayer caused Habakkuk further agony of heart, leading to the second dialogue (1:12—2:20). God's plan of action seemed to contradict the prophet's theology (1:12-17). The prophet had looked upon God as an eternally holy Person who must judge the unjust and acquit the righteous. Why, then, did God seem to be involving Himself in a compromising situation? The Chaldeans were far more wicked than Judah, and much more in need of judgment. How could God justify chastening Israel at the hands of those who were more culpable? As Habakkuk wrestled with that dilemma, he waited upon the Lord to reveal His will to Him (2:1).

In revealing His will to Habakkuk, God showed that His righteousness would be vindicated in the downfall of the Chaldean (or Babylonian) empire. His answer was in three parts.

9. M. F. Unger, *Unger's Commentary on the Old Testament* (Chicago: Moody, 1981), 2:1895.
10. Gaebelein, *Four Minor Prophets.* p. 141.

First there was reassurance that He was in control of the situation (2:2-3). Then there was recognition on the part of God of the wicked character of the Chaldeans and of the faithful character of the righteous remnant (2:4). Finally, there was divine reason for the judgment of the Chaldeans (2:5-20). That reason included indictments for five distinct sins: proud ambition (2:5-8), covetousness (2:9-11), ruthlessness and cruelty (2:12-14), debauchery (2:15-17), and idolatry (2:18-19).

Finally, God's holiness was vindicated, and the prophet was able to reconcile his theology with God's actions (2:20).

Habakkuk devoted chapter 3 to praise. The prophet's vision of God's plan and purpose had been broadened. It included not only the immediate future but also the fuller scope of God's dealings with His people as well as with the nations of the earth. In the final section, therefore, Habakkuk consoled his people, who were suffering from violence and injustice, and encouraged them with the same confidence God had inspired in him. He reviewed God's faithfulness by drawing illustrations from Israel's past history (3:3-15).

In the conclusion (3:16-19), Habakkuk caught a glimpse of the glorious faithfulness of God and brought it into living focus so that he and those in Jerusalem with him would rely upon the Lord during the coming time of tribulation (see especially 3:16, 19). In doing so, he showed that trials and perplexity were not incompatible with trust in God.

IV. OUTLINE OF THE BOOK

2

I. THE COMPLAINT OF HABAKKUK, 1:1—2:20

In his book *When Bad Things Happen to Good People,* Rabbi Harold Kushner describes his own feelings when soon after his son Aaron's second birthday, he and his wife learned that Aaron had progeria. That rare disease would cause their son to age rapidly and die in his early teens.

As painful as the news of Aaron's condition was, nothing could be compared to the suffering of the next twelve years as their son aged before their eyes. During this time of acute trial, the question continuously thrust upon them was, Why? Why did Aaron have to suffer? He was a happy, innocent child. Why should he suffer physical and psychological pain every day of his life?[1]

In keeping with many people who have benefited from a religious upbringing, Kushner and his wife had been reared to believe that God was an all-wise, all-powerful parent figure who would treat them as their earthly parents had done, or even better. What they endured during Aaron's lingering illness all but shattered those beliefs.

After recounting the events, the rabbi writes:

> There is only one question which really matters: why do bad things happen to good people? All other theological conversation is intellectually diverting. . . . Virtually every meaningful conversation I have ever had with people on the subject of God and religion has either started with this question, or gotten around to it before long. Not only the troubled man or woman who has just come

1. Harold S. Kushner, *When Bad Things Happen to Good People* (New York: Schocken, 1981), p. 2.

from a discouraging diagnosis at the doctor's office, but the college student who tells me that he has decided there is no God, or the total stranger who comes up to me at a party just when I am ready to ask the hostess for my coat, and says, "I hear you're a rabbi; how can you believe that . . . "—they all have one thing in common. They are all troubled by the unfair distribution of suffering in the world.

The misfortunes of good people are not only a problem to the people who suffer and to their families. They are a problem to everyone who wants to believe in a just and fair and livable world. They inevitably raise questions about the goodness, the kindness, even the existence of God.[2]

All who suffer are likely to ask the same question, and those in the helping professions—doctors, nurses, psychologists, counselors, social workers—who confront the evidences of human suffering day after day find themselves in the same position as Kushner. Fortunately, God anticipated that need and years ago worked through the life and experiences of Habakkuk to provide a satisfactory answer to the problem of injustice and suffering. That solution lies in the text of Habakkuk.

INTRODUCTION, 1:1

Habakkuk opened his prophecy with a sentence that commanded attention. That sentence was in reality a superscription or title to the entire book. The words prefaced the prophet's own struggle with the prevalence of sin and man's inhumanity to man. They also prepared the prophet's listeners for what was to follow.

The first word of the text *măśśā'*, "burden, oracle," was used in nonprophetic passages of a load to be lifted (cf. Ex. 23:5; Num. 11:11), but in prophetic passages such as the book of Habakkuk, it announced heavy judgments upon the people.

2. Ibid., pp. 5-6.

As Keil has shown, "*massa* never occurs in the title [of a prophecy] except when it is evidently grave and full of weight and labour."[3]

Habakkuk's "burden" was connected with the next word, *ḥāzâ*, "envision," namely, that which God caused him "to see." Once again, the prophet took a word out of its ordinary use and applied it to the extraordinary conditions of prophetic vision (cf., Isa. 13:1; Nah. 1:1).

In addition, as was pointed out in the previous section, Habakkuk referred to himself as a "prophet." There can be little doubt that he belonged to a special group of individuals to whom the Lord communicated His will by means of dreams and visions, and who was charged with the task of communicating God's message to His people.

The "burden" that made up Habakkuk's prophecy took the form of a dialogue. The structure was simple. Habakkuk, who had been oppressed by a sense of the prevalence of iniquity, unburdened his heart to the Lord (1:2-4). In answer to his passionate entreaty, God revealed His plans to His prophet (1:5-11). That revelation was followed by a second dialogue (1:12—2:20), in which God's righteousness in Israel's chastisement was vindicated (1:12—2:1) and the fall of the Chaldeans was predicted (2:2-20).

A. THE FIRST DIALOGUE, 1:2-11

As Habakkuk began to pour out his heart to the Lord, he gave expression to his perplexity: How could God allow lawlessness to prevail among His people and the righteous to be exploited and oppressed? In other words, "Why did bad things happen to good people?"

In his commentary, S. R. Driver places Habakkuk's complaint in the context of the times. He points out that Josiah's reformation, less than a decade and a half earlier, was not only a memory. Jehoiakim was a selfish and tyrannical ruler. At a time when the country was impoverished by the collection of tribute imposed by Pharaoh Neco, Jehoiakim developed a pas-

---

3. C. F. Keil, *Bible Commentary on the Old Testament, The Minor Prophets* (Grand Rapids: Eerdmans, n.d.), 2:55.

sion for regal grandeur. Jeremiah records that he built, by means of forced, unpaid labor, a spacious place, "paneled with cedar and painted with vermilion" (Jer. 22:13-17). Furthermore, he abused his position as the vassal of Egypt and indulged in the vices of oriental despots. His eyes and his heart were set upon dishonest gain, and he shed innocent blood from one quarter of Jerusalem to another. As a consequence, those in positions of power in Judah abused their authority and indulged in lawlessness, injustice, dishonesty, and oppression (cf. Jer. 11:10; 14:7, 10-12, 20).[4]

With the context of the times in mind, the prophet's prayer can be considered.

1. GOD'S INACTIVITY IN ISRAEL'S AFFAIRS, 1:2-4

As with other great men of God, Habakkuk's recourse in the face of injustice was to seek God's face in prayer. His prayer fell into two related parts: God's apparent indifference to his former entreaties (1:2), and God's apparent indifference to Israel's sin (1:3-4).

a. God's Indifference to Habakkuk's Prayers, 1:2

Habakkuk's words, "How long, O LORD" (NASB) seem to indicate that he had prayed about these matters before. God's apparent indifference had only increased the burden for the downtrodden that the prophet felt. This time, however, his entreaty was more fervent than before. His cry *ḥāmās*, "violence!" was an adverbial accusative. It placed justifiable emphasis upon the intensity of the prophet's petition. He had observed the appalling conditions of God's people and could no longer tolerate the cry of the oppressed. Therefore, he poured out his heart to the Lord, beseeching Him in the most fervent of terms to intervene on behalf of His people.

Habakkuk's prayer revealed his true humanity. He was frustrated and bewildered. Daily he saw the plight of the poor. He had petitioned the Lord to help them, and now, in frustration, he reproved God for not intervening and vindicating the righteous (1:2d).

4. S. R. Driver, *The Minor Prophets,* The Century Bible (Edinburgh: T. C. and E. C. Black, 1960), pp. 51-52.

b. *God's Indifference to Israel's Sin,* 1:3-4

To those not acquainted with the grief and suffering of others who are being victimized and exploited, Habakkuk's prayer sounds impertinent, if not sacriligious. Habakkuk gave an explanation of his deep anxiety of heart in 1:3-4. In discharging his God-appointed duties to the nation, he had continually to look upon iniquity. He had seen the wickedness of those in positions of power and influence. With an inner helplessness, he had viewed destruction, violence, perversion of justice, and the oppression of the poor. The sorrow he felt on account of what he had seen had not been alleviated by any evidence of God's care or concern.

That Habakkuk was right to expect God to intervene had been made clear in the writings of the prophets who had preceded him. God had chosen Jerusalem as the place where His name would be established. It had been asserted through Isaiah, during Manasseh's reign, that violence would not be heard again in the land, nor would devastation or destruction occur within its borders. The walls of Jerusalem would be symbols of "salvation," her gates would be emblems of "praise" (Isa. 60:18, NASB; cf. Isaiah 61:3, 11*b*), and the city would become "a praise in the earth" (Isa. 62:6-7, NASB).

What Habakkuk witnessed all about him, however, was in marked contrast to what he had been led to expect. And what was even more perplexing was the fact that God appeared to tolerate (*tăbbîṭ,* "to look at") evil, strife, and contention (1:3). Furthermore, the law which God had established so that His people would enjoy a righteous government had become ineffective (*pûg,* "chilled, benumbed"), and as a consequence justice never prevailed (1:4*a*). The wicked circumvented the righteous requirements of the Lord and twisted and manipulated the law to serve their own selfish purposes.[5]

God's apparent silence should not have caused Habakkuk to believe that He was indifferent. As will be found in the next

---

5. F. A. Tatford in his commentary, *Prophet of the Watchtower: An Exposition of Habakkuk,* vol. 2 of *The Minor Prophets* (Minneapolis: Klock and Klock, 1983), 19-20, refers to Robert Anderson's book, *The Silence of God* (Sir Robert Anderson Library, 1978), pp. 61-62, for a clear and definitive analysis of the recurrence of such events in history.

section, the Lord had been working behind the scenes in answer to His servant's prayers. Instead of alleviating the oppressed, as the prophet expected, He was going to judge the oppressors. His judgment, though long delayed, was certain. As Anne of Austria once remarked to Cardinal Richelieu, "God does not pay at the end of every day, my Lord Cardinal, but at the end He pays."

2. GOD'S REVELATION OF HIS ACTIVITY, 1:5-11

a. His Intention to Chasten His People, 1:5

While the Lord had not answered the former complaints of His prophet, now He responded to Habakkuk's importunate plea. The Lord's words were startling. The Hebrew text begins with "See . . . ." That is followed by "behold! be astonished! . . . [and] wonder!" The Lord did not respond to the prophet's question, "Why?" He is sovereign. He does not need to explain or apologize for His actions. He remains the great "I AM THAT I AM" (Ex. 3:14, KJV). Men cannot understand His dealings with them, nor do men have the wisdom to counsel Him regarding His actions. In grace, however, God provides brief intimations of His plans—of events that are taking place behind the stage of history. Far from being insensitive to the trials of His people, He orchestrates events and circumstances that can only be described in superlative terms (Heb. *tmh tmh*, "to be exceedingly amazed," 1:5*a*).

Following His words to Habakkuk, "Look among the nations! Observe! Be astonished! Wonder!" (1:5, NASB) the Lord informed His servant that, far from being indifferent to the events and circumstances surrounding His people, He was going to chasten them. His plan of action was such that people would not believe it even if they were told (1:5*b*). His design was to reprove his people for their unbelief and to discipline them for breaking His law. He then told Habakkuk that the judgment He planned to bring to pass would take place "in your days," in other words, during the lifetime of the prophet and the people then living in Jerusalem.

What does such a statement reveal about the nature of God

and His dealings with mankind? The words were designed to
bring comfort. In our darkest hour, when we are prone to feel
that the Lord has forsaken us, we are inclined to think of the
lines of James Russell Lowell:

> Careless seems the great Avenger;
> History's pages but record
> One death-grapple in the darkness 'twixt
> Old systems and the Word;
> *Truth forever on the scaffold,*
> *Wrong forever on the throne,—*
> Yet that scaffold sways the future,
> And, behind the dim unknown,
> Standeth God within the shadow,
> Keeping watch above His own.[6]

We should remember that God has not lost control. He is
still in command of events. It is only a lack of perception that
makes Him seem inactive. His activity extends from one
generation to the next, and as Habakkuk was soon to find out,
will culminate in the millenial kingdom.

Ever since Merodach-Baladin had seized the throne of
Babylon (721 B.C.), God had been at work preparing the Chaldeans to punish Assyria. Having revealed His plans regarding
His people (1:5), the Lord proceeded to show to Habakkuk
more of His purpose in the Chaldeans as instruments to
chasten Israel (1:6-11). He gave the prophet a full account of
the chastisement to come (1:6) as well as a preview of Chaldean
despotism (1:7-11).

b. *His Instrument to Chasten His People,* 1:6-11
   (1) Foreview of Israel's Destruction, 1:6-7

The Chaldeans, whom the Lord was in the process of "raising up," were originally a semi-nomadic desert tribe. They had
settled in southern Babylonia, where they gradually increased
in power. In 626 B.C., Nebopolassar came to the throne and

---

6. *The Complete Poetical Works of James Russell Lowell,* ed. H. E. Scud-
   der (Boston: Houghton Mifflin, n.d.), p. 67.

founded a dynasty that ultimately dominated the world of that day. His son Nebuchadnezzar would defeat Pharaoh Neco in the battle of Carchemish in 605 B.C. and succeed his father as king of the neo-Babylonian empire. The description given in 1:6-11 was an accurate picture of the rapacious cruelty of the Babylonian horde.

The Lord used various descriptive terms to present the Chaldeans (or Babyonians). He portrayed them as a "fierce and impetuous" people (3:6, NASB; *măr*, "cruel, bitter"; and *nĭmhār*, "hurried, rash") who swept through the land, pillaging and plundering on their way. They took possession of houses that were not theirs (cf. Jer. 8:10), and they were feared and dreaded for their cruelty and heartlessness.

The Lord also used the words *'āyōm*, "formidable, terrible," and *nôrā*, "dreaded, feared" to describe the Babylonians. They were a people capable of fulfilling to the utmost the prophecy of Jeremiah 1:15. With arrogance and presumption, they imposed judgment on the kings and peoples they subdued. Their self-assumed authority was administered with scant thought of any reprisal from, or any accountability to, a higher power (1:7). They were a law unto themselves and promoted whatever they desired (Jer. 39:5-9). Such arrogance and imperiousness resulted in abuse of power, rather than its proper use.

What history revealed in the case of the Chaldeans has been practiced numerous times since. All one need do is reflect upon the activities of Germany at the beginning of World War II, or of Russia in more recent years. Poland, Holland, Czechoslovakia, Hungary, and Afghanistan have suffered in much the same way as Judah of old. Although God has seemingly permitted such unbridled aggression to go unpunished, the fact remains that God eventually calls each nation to account for its actions.

(2) Preview of the Chaldean's Destruction, 1:8-11

The picture God gave Habakkuk of the Chaldean invasion was expressed through a series of vivid metaphors (1:8-11). The Lord compared the agility and mobility of the Babylonian cavalry men to the swiftness of leopards (1:8*a*). When they came against Judah, they would kill for the sake of killing, and would loot, rape, and spread fear and terror to every corner of the land. The Lord described the Babylonians as being "keener than evening wolves" (1:8*b*; cf. Jer. 5:6; Zeph. 3:3) who are more fierce and more cunning on account of their hunger. Those lean animals could easily be visualized coming out of the woods and caves in the mountains toward dusk and then entering villages to devour greedily anything and everything they saw.

The Lord portrayed the Chaldean invasion under the figure of "horsemen" come from afar, who fanned out in all directions. He likened the Chaldeans to birds of prey that swoop down upon the victims they plan to consume (1:8*c*; cf. Ezek. 17:3; Hos. 8:1).

A reader might believe that a conquering army would be satisfied with the plunder derived from sacking villages and towns. In the case of the Babylonians, however, they were not. "All of them come for violence" (1:9*c*, NASB). Their goal was savage and ruthless oppression. Their faces were set forward with such eagerness and anticipation that they rushed onward to newer conquests, taking one village after another and gathering captives with greater ease than they would scoop up handfuls of sand by the sea (cf. 1:9*b*).

Nebuchadnezzar wrote of his campaign in the following words:

> At that time, the Lebanon, the [Cedar] Mountain, the luxurious forest of Marduk . . . over which a foreign enemy was ruling and robbing (it of) its riches—its people were scattered, had fled to a far (away region). Trusting in the power of my lords [*i.e.*, my gods] Nebo and Marduk, I organized [my army] for [an expedition] to the Lebanon. I made that country happy by eradicating its enemy everywhere.[7]

The Babylonians mocked the kings of the various provinces

7. J. B. Pritchard, ed., *Ancient Near Eastern Texts Relating to the Old Testament,* 2d ed. (Princeton: Princeton U. 1955), p. 307.

through which they passed (1:10*a*). Once captured, kings were treated cruelly. It was a Chaldean custom to put captive rulers in cages and exhibit them as public spectacles. Frequently their eyes were put out (cf., 2 Kings 25:7) and they became a gazing stock (*mišhāq,* "to scorn, to laugh at") of the people (1:10*a*). Fortified cities were treated with the same contemptuous derision (*śhq,* "to laugh at, to make fun of"). Earthen ramps were constructed against each such cities, making their capture relatively easy (1:10*b*).

When they had attained the initial victory, the attitude (*rûăh,* "spirit") of the invaders changed. Their thoughts turned quickly to new areas of conquest. Like the wind, they passed on (1:11). Nothing, it appeared, could restrain them. In 1:11, however, the Lord gave an intimation of His attitude toward their wanton destruction. "They will be held guilty," he observed, NASB. Their pride and arrogance were merely preparing them for their own destruction (cf. Prov. 16:18; Jer. 2:3; cf. Dan. 4:16, 30-34).

As we have seen from Nebuchadnezzar's own annals, his soldiers attributed their strength to the gods they worshiped. That they did so will be enlarged upon in the section that follows. As the material covered so far is reviewed, however, it is fitting to take note of the familiar adage, "Power corrupts and absolute power corrupts absolutely." History is replete with illustrations of those who have abused the powers given them by God. In turn, they have been judged, and all they sought to erect has come to nought.

That principle was illustrated by Percy Bysshe Shelley who, during his travels in Egypt, saw lying in the sands of the desert the huge colossus that Ramases II had erected to himself. Transliterating the name, he wrote the poem "Ozymandias."

> "My name is Ozymandias, king of kings:
> Look on my works, ye Mighty, and despair!"
> Nothing beside remains. Round the decay
> Of that colossal wreck, Boundless and bare
> The lone and level sands stretch far away.[8]

8. *The Complete Poetical Works of Shelley,* ed. G. E. Woodberry (Boston: Houghton Mifflin, 1901), p. 356.

God is repulsed by pride and haughtiness and has promised to bring to nought the works of the arrogant and insolent (Prov. 16:18).

Such circumstances do not belong in remote antiquity, for God is unchanging. What we sow, we reap (Gal. 6:7-8). Corporations and churches, cartels and educational institutions have found to their chagrin that pride, oppression, and exploitation, however subtly practiced, have paved the way for their destruction just as surely as the greed and avarice of the rich and powerful in Jerusalem sowed the seeds of Judah's demise.[9]

9. Cf. P. Solman and T. Friedman, *Life and Death on the Corporate Battle-field* (New York: Simon & Schuster, 1982), and the equally enlightening book by T. J. Peters and R. H. Waterman, Jr., *In Search of Excellence: Lessons from America's Best Run Companies* (New York: Harper and Row, 1982), a work that underscores (albeit unintentionally) numerous biblical principles. See also C. J. Barber and G. H. Strauss, *Leadership: The Dynamics of Success* (Greenwood, S.C.: Attic, 1982).

3

I. THE COMPLAINT OF HABAKKUK, 1:1—2:20 (*CONTINUED*)

The first dialogue in Habakkuk (1:1-11) began with the prophet's complaint about the sins of his people and God's apparent indifference. God graciously showed His prophet that, far from being indifferent, He was planning to chasten the people. At that very moment He was at work bringing the Chaldean empire to a position of power. In His own good time, He would use them as His "rod" to discipline wayward Judah.

The second dialogue in Habakkuk (1:12—2:20) centered on a more intense problem: How could a holy and righteous God use a people as evil as the Chaldeans as His instrument of chastisement?

B. THE SECOND DIALOGUE, 1:12—2:20

1. GOD'S RIGHTEOUSNESS IN ISRAEL'S CHASTISEMENT, 1:12—2:1

As Habakkuk received God's revelation of impending judgment, his earlier problems paled into insignificance before the theological conundrum posed by God's use of the Chaldeans. The words of the Lord in 1:5-11 seemed out of keeping with His love for and election of His covenant people (Gen. 12:3; 18:18; 26:4; 28:14). Taken at face value, the revelation Habakkuk received seemed to imply the destruction of God's people and the obliteration of the covenant.

Habakkuk's response to the Lord fell into three sections: (1) the instrument of God's choice (1:12-13*a*); (2) the consistency of God's plan (1:13*b*-17); and (3) the dilemma of God's prophet (2:1).

a. The Instrument of God's Choice, 1:12-13a

Habakkuk's statement in 1:12 was a mixture of bewilderment and faith. In contrast to the Chaldean's belief in their "god," Habakkuk believed that the Lord was eternal. He was from everlasting. Habakkuk's words also implied his own personal faith (note the emphasis on "my").

That Habakkuk made the propositional statement of 1:12 in the form of a question did not imply doubt. It was the Hebrew way of making an affirmative comment.

Habakkuk's humanity was clearly in evidence as he described his feelings. His emotions surfaced. His cry, "We will not die," was tantamount to saying, "That cannot be! That would contradict, O Lord, your Own nature and everything I have come to believe about You." The prophet then repeated what he thought he had heard God say. The prophet's remonstrance was based upon His belief in the unchangeable character of God (1:12). Because God was from everlasting, Habakkuk believed He could sustain His people through all the trials and vicissitudes that faced them. He was mindful of God's covenant and believed that He would bring it to fruition regardless of what might happen in the immediate future. Such assurance has been of great comfort to all who have faced affliction or misunderstanding, tribulation or loss.

b. The Consistency of God's Plan, 1:13b-17

In 1:13-17 Habakkuk reviewed his own belief in God as well as what God has just revealed to him. Because God was of purer eyes than to behold iniquity (1:13; cf. Ps. 11:4-6; 34:16), Habakkuk failed to see how He could use a nation more wicked than Israel to chasten Israel (cf. Jer. 12:1-2). From a human perspective it appeared as if God were looking with favor upon those who dealt treacherously.

Habakkuk's dilemma was similar to that of the psalmist who pondered the same things (cf. Ps. 37; 49; 73). And Habakkuk, who had previously reproved the Lord for being silent when he called out to Him about the sins of his people, now reproved God for standing by while "the wicked swallow up those more righteous than they" (1:13, NASB). His statement implied that the righteous would suffer with the guilty, a development he thought was inconsistent with the idea of a holy and just God.

As Habakkuk continued his complaint (1:14ff.), he asked

why the Lord appeared to have made men like the fish of the sea, or like creeping things without a ruler. Their vulnerability made them easy prey for whoever wanted to take advantage of them.

Having introduced a fishing motif, Habakkuk developed it in several figures of speech describing the ways in which the Chaldeans would take advantage of God's people. They would use the (fish) hook, the net, and the dragnet to capture and ensnare those in Judah. They would employ every conceivable means to take advantage of God's people. Because they had no real leader over them, God's people would be like so many fish caught in a net and drawn to the shore against their will.

Those who caught them would "rejoice and [be] glad" (1:15, NASB). They would gather far more than they could eat, gorge themselves to the full, and take delight in the cruelty they inflicted upon the helpless.

With a touch of irony, Habakkuk portrayed the Chaldeans offering sacrifices to their gods (1:16). All of the Babylonian deities, at one time or another, were pictured holding or dragging a net in which they had captured their enemies. The Babylonians depicted their enemies as squirming about like fish, seeking for a means of escape. The net, it would appear, served the Babylonians as a symbol of power and sovereignty. The more people they drew into their nets, the greater their joy was. They then offered sacrifices to the gods whom they worshiped and bowed down before those who they believed had given them success.

In 1:17 Habakkuk summarized the point he had been making. He asked if the Chaldeans would indeed make an end of God's people ("empty their net") and continue to "slay [the different] nations without sparing" them (NASB). The question was left unanswered. The reader, however, can sense the prophet's dilemma. All that he knew of the Chaldeans and all that God had just revealed to him seemed to indicate that they would. Yet Habakkuk believed that it would be inconsistent with His character for God to allow such a thing to happen.

The predicament that Habakkuk faced was not an uncommon one. Instead of having his initial problem resolved, the revelation he was given only served to raise new questions in his mind. As will be evident, his views of God were right (cf. Ps. 82; Isa. 57:15), but his perspective was too limited. He had looked for the punishment of the wicked so that the prosperity of his people could be assured, but God, who knew the end from the beginning, looked for the punishment of Habakkuk's people so that they could be restored to fellowship. The truths enunciated in Isaiah (cf. Isa. 15:9; 60:18) applied particularly to the millennial age as opposed to Habakkuk's day. In time, the Lord would lead His prophet to an understanding of that perspective.

c. *The Dilemma of God's Prophets,* 2:1

Habakkuk's response to the new revelation can be described as a fine example of patience in the midst of perplexity or as meekness in the face of expected reproof. If it was patience, then 2:1 expressed the prophet's determination to wait patiently for God's answer. The prophet could be compared to a watchman on a battlement stationing himself on a rampart and there preparing himself for whatever the Lord might reveal to him (2:1).

Other prophets grappled with issues they could not understand (cf. Dan. 9:2, 11, 13; 1 Pet. 1:10-12). In Habakkuk's case, however, he is fully aware that his words merited divine reproof. He fully expected God to censure him for his attitude. Realizing how bold he had been in God's presence, Habakkuk found a secluded place, perhaps in his own room near an open window or else in a solitary part of the wall surrounding Jerusalem. There he waited for God's reproof (2:1).

The words that followed (2:2-20) were an evidence of God's grace. He did not reprove His prophet. Neither did He answer the question why? Instead, He boldly announced His intention to hold accountable and punish the Chaldeans for their pride, arrogance, and unbridled cruelty.

2. GOD'S RIGHTEOUSNESS IN THE CHALDEAN'S DOWNFALL, 2:2-20

a. *His Warning to Israel,* (2:2-4)

The warning the Lord revealed to Habakkuk fell into three

sections: (1) declaration of the vision (2:2); (2) the certainty of chastisement (2:3); and (3) provision for God's people (2:4).

(1) Declaration of God's Wisdom, 2:2

As Habakkuk waited quietly in some secluded place far from the pressures of city life, the word of the Lord came to him. Instead of the expected reproof, he was told to "write the vision." The word the Lord used for vision was $\underline{h}\bar{a}z\hat{o}n$, "a revelation," divine truth supernaturally given. The vision, though brief, was far reaching in its scope and was of momentous importance. It described God's provision for the safety of His people and it underscored the principle of His unchanging operation. Habakkuk was told to "write" the vision, that is, to inscribe it upon tablets and place them in a public place, possibly in the gate of the Temple, so that those who read them might be alerted to the coming judgment.

There are those who insist that what the prophets wrote only became the "word of the Lord" when it was formally accepted into the canon of Scripture. They claim that the "canon of the prophets" was not closed until third century B.C., and that, therefore, what Habakkuk wrote was "officially recognized" as God's revelation to His people after it was too late for those living at the time to do anything to save themselves.

Such persons overlook the last portion of 2:2, "That the one who reads it may run," a statement that assumes that God's Word was recognized as being authoritative the moment it was given, a position conservatives have always held. It did not have to wait for some council to be called in order for it to receive canonical status. The vision the Lord was about to give Habakkuk was intended as a warning from God. Those pious souls in Jerusalem who read what God told Habakkuk to write were to heed what it said and flee the city before it was invaded by the Chaldeans.

(2) Recognition of God's Will, 2:3

In 2:3 the Lord emphasized that the vision Habakkuk was to record dealt with certainties. It was for an "appointed time" (NASB). The evil of which Habakkuk had complained was about to be judged. Punishment of the wicked would be on schedule. Outward circumstances might seem to indicate that God's judgment was long delayed, but even as they spoke, God's plan was hastening (lit., panting) "towards its goal." It would not fail. Therefore, Habakkuk was instructed to wait for it.

The mark of God's grace implicit in that warning was given as well in Ezekiel 9:4-6, 8. Those who did not flee in response to the divine warning and yet were righteous were to have a special "mark" placed on them so that they would be spared during the coming invasion. God's compassion and loving-kindness would be evident even in chastisement.

(3) Provision for God's People, 2:4

With 2:4 there came a change in the subject of God's revelation. The vision being communicated to Habakkuk turned from God's people to the proud invader. The emphasis upon "his soul" (NASB) was a Hebraism describing the haughty arrogance of the Chaldeans, who were spoken of collectively as a single person. The Chaldeans were inflated with pride. They were supercilious, self-sufficient, and authoritarian. By way of contrast, "the righteous [one, or man] will live by his faith" (2:4*c,* NASB).

That statement, comprising only three words in the original text, contained a seminal truth further amplified in three key books of the New Testament. In Romans 1:17 the reference was to belief in God in contrast to the unbelief of the pagan world. In Galatians 3:11 the emphasis was on the principle of faith in contrast to the principle of law (which made nothing perfect). And in Hebrews 10:38 the stress was on the confidence the life of faith gave the believer in the face of suffering and persecution. Living by faith was in marked contrast to walking by sight.

Gaebelein shows that in the first half of 2:4 the Lord compressed into a pithy statement a key to understanding the philosophy of history. In the second half of the verse the Lord described a solution to the way in which those who are righteous may live in an unrighteous and unjust world.[1] Such weighty matters should neither be forgotten nor ignored.

The truth contained in 2:4c was designed to bring comfort to believers. It showed that faith (*'emûnâ*, "trust") in God was the key to consistent living, even though violence abounded and justice was perverted (1:2-4). Today that short statement helps believers to persevere even though God chastens them (1:5-11) and they cannot understand His ways (1:12-17). It provides a solution to the doubt they sometimes feel in His all-wise providence (2:1-3), and helps them to understand his righteous judgments (2:4-20). In the final analysis, faith provides the key to understanding the Lord's sovereign purpose, and it leads men to worship (3:1-19).

In the portion of the prophecy immediately following 2:4, the Lord described those whose lives were not characterized by faith. They were overbearing and filled with avarice. They engaged in tyranny and were motivated by policies of self-aggrandizement. Such people wrote their own obituary. Although their strategies might succeed for a time, they carried with them the seeds of destruction. Ultimately, the wicked would fall under the weight of their iniquities (2:5).[2]

While it might be expected that 2:5 could be applied to different world powers, the principle of the verse is also applicable to state and city government; to corporations, schools, hospitals; and to institutions of all types, Christian and non-Christian. Arrogant leaders, wherever they might be, have no right to run roughshod over human feelings and exploit individuals for the sake of personal gain.

In vindicating His ways with mankind, God described the oppressed nations and peoples as taking up a "taunt-song" against their oppressors (2:6, NASB).

b. His Punishment of the Chaldeans, 2:5-19

In order to explain why bad things happen to good people, the Lord gave Habakkuk a vision of His justice: the Chaldeans

1. F. E., Gaebelein, *Four Minor Prophets* (Chicago: Moody, 1970), p. 166.
2. Ibid., p. 167.

would be used to chasten God's people. Then the Lord demonstrated His righteousness further by pronouncing five woes upon the oppressors. In doing so He showed that the sweep of history extended beyond a single generation. His grace would be manifested from one generation to another, as He moved steadily forward to accomplish His goal.

In the process, those who had become intoxicated by conquest and had roamed far and wide in order to heap up riches for themselves (and had plundered people unnecessarily, cf. 2 Kings 14:10; Prov. 27:20; 30:16; Isa. 5:14) would find that the day of retribution came speedily. Ironically, those who were lovers of wine would find that their ruin was accomplished on account of it (cf. Dan. 5).[3]

The five woes that detailed the judgment upon the Chaldeans were given in a series of strophes of three verses each. While 2:6a constituted a summary statement, the woes taken together provided a striking example of the manner in which ungodly administrations sowed the seeds of their own destruction (cf. 2:4a).[4]

Inasmuch as Babylon was soon to rise to the height of its power and would not be overthrown for another seventy years (until 539 B.C.), the scope of what God revealed to His prophet in 2:5-19 was significant.

God showed Habakkuk that Babylon's fate would take place at the hands of the peoples they had plundered. The Babylonians would be mocked by a "parable" (*melîṣâ*, "satirical ditty") and a "mockery" (NASB; from *hîdôt*, "mocking insinuation")—a kind of "jeering song couched in ambiguous or double-meaning terminology"[5] sung by those they had once conquered (2:6).

---

3. The excessive drinking habits of the Babylonians have been described by G. Rawlinson, *Five Monarchies of the Ancient Eastern World* (London: John Murray, 1871), 3:19. See also H. W. F. Saggs, *The Greatness That Was Babylon* (New York: Hawthorn, 1962).
4. B. L. Montgomery, *The Path to Leadership* (London: Collins, 1961), 9-19. See also C. J. Barber and G. H. Strauss, *Leadership: The Dynamics of Success* (Greenwood, S.C.: Attic, 1982), pp. 12-24.
5. M. F. Unger, *Unger's Commentary on the Old Testament* (Chicago: Moody, 1981), 2:1906.

(1) For Their Ambition, 2:5-8

The first woe described the punishment of the Chaldeans for their ambition (2:5-8). It specifically highlighted their greed, robbery, acts of vandalism, and avarice. Emphasis was placed on the fact that they had increased their possessions by unlawful means. They had used violence to acquire what their hearts had desired (1:6b). Then, like a crafty and unscrupulous money lender, they had extorted interest from those whom they had plundered (2:6c).

In the vision God gave Habakkuk, the prophet saw the "creditors" suddenly rising up against the Chaldeans (2:7, NASB). The tables were turned, and all that the Chaldeans had acquired as a consequence of their conquests became the spoils of war of those whom they had oppressed[6] (cf. Isa. 13:19-22).

The ruins of Babylon today bear testimony to the truth of God's Word and to the fate that overtook the once proud city.[7] As has been pointed out by different writers, various superstitions that prevent them from pitching their tents near the site of the ancient city are current among the Arabs. Furthermore, the character of the soil prevents the growth of vegetation suitable for the pasturing of flocks. The ruins that remain consist of caves and holes occupied only by wild animals. At night their cries reverberate between the walls, and human beings are seldom seen in the vicinity (Isa. 13:17-22; 14:22-23; Jer. 50:29-32, 35-37, 39-40; 51:1-64).

(2) For Their Covetousness, 2:9-11

The first woe was pronounced against the Chaldeans for their inordinate greed; the second woe concerned their covetousness (2:9-11). From the original text it seems clear that the Babylonians desired to assert dominance and authority over the nations.

Although the thrust of the verses may well have been directed against Nebuchadnezzar and his desire to establish his dynasty in perpetuity, a more general application of the truth

6. Ibid.
7. H. W. F. Saggs, "Babylon," in *Archaeology and Old Testament Study,* ed. D. W. Thomas (Oxford: Clarendon, 1967), pp. 39-56.

presented could have been to those under his command as well. They, too, had sought to enrich themselves by means of plunder and, in keeping with the precedent and example set by their leader, had engaged in policies of covetousness and self-aggrandizement. They had sought to establish themselves securely and had not hesitated to cut off other peoples and nations so that they could acquire material possessions.

The vision given Habakkuk was of an eagle setting its nest in high, inaccessible place. Keil points out that, as

> the eagle builds its nest on high, to protect it from harm (cf. Job 39:27), so does the Chaldean seek to elevate and strengthen his rule by robbery and plunder, that it may never be wrested from his family again.[8]

Another Old Testament prophet, Obadiah, described a similar desire for security (Obad. 1:4).

The well laid plans of aggression were, however, to bring calamity upon the oppressors. Their strategies to ensure security would fail, and they would be cut off (2:10). Having planned to build their own power and glory through the destruction of different peoples, they were to see their cruel schemes backfire. In the very act of cutting off other nations, they were "sinning against [themselves]," for rather than provide them security, the nations would cry out for vengeance against them (NASB).

Even the stones and the timbers with which the Babylonians had built houses and palaces would call out for vengeance (2:11). The spoils of war by which the nation and its people had enriched themselves would witness against them.

(3) For Their Ruthlessness, 2:12-14

While the Chaldeans were to be judged for ambition and covetousness, they were also to be judged for other crimes against humanity. The third woe pronounced upon the Chaldeans was for their ruthlessness (2:12-14). They were to be

---

8. C. F. Keil, *Bible Commentary on the Old Testament: The Minor Prophets* (Grand Rapids: Eerdmans, n.d.), 2:83.

punished for their iniquitous building programs. Cities had been built with forced labor. Palaces had been erected at the expense of subjected peoples who had been pressed into slavery. Blood had been shed unnecessarily (cf. 2:12; Mic. 3:10; Nah. 3:1). Nebuchadnezzar had carried on a relentless policy of beautifying Babylon. In light of God's righteousness, his plans were seen to have been at the expense of the poor and the defenseless and his city established by iniquity.

Of those inscriptions from Nebuchadnezzar's reign that have come down to us, most of them describe his building projects. The gigantic walls of the city, its ramparts, gates, fortifications, ziggurat, palace, and hanging gardens are proverbial.[9]

As impregnable as the city might have seemed from a human standpoint, the Lord had decreed its destruction (Jer. 51:58; cf. Dan. 2:36-45). By way of contrast, that which God intended to establish would last forever. When the Jews returned from Babylon under the administration of the Medes and Persians and settled again in the "Promised Land," they would rebuild the Temple. That resettlement would prefigure the ultimate and final establishment of the millennial kingdom under the Lord Jesus Christ. With that revelation, Habakkuk began to see how the prophecies of Isaiah of the future glory of Israel harmonized with God's plan and purpose for the nations.

At one time Habakkuk might have expected Isaiah's prophecies to be fulfilled in his own lifetime. Now his initial quest for understanding had been enlarged to the point that he grasped something of the magnitude of God's purpose: God's plan included the whole earth. One day the whole earth would "be filled with the knowledge of the glory of the LORD, As the waters cover the sea" (2:14, NASB). Such a rule of righteousness would be in marked contrast to the reign of the Chaldeans, whose ambition, covetousness, and ruthlessness led them to debauch the nations.

(4) For Their Debauchery, 2:15-17

The fourth woe (2:15-17) followed close upon the heels of

9. C. F. Pfeiffer, ed., *The Biblical World* (Grand Rapids: Baker, 1966), pp. 124-33.

that brief glimpse of what the Lord had in mind for the far-distant future. Woe was pronounced upon the Chaldeans because they were satiated with shame. Their evil conduct was a distinct contrast to the glory of God's kingdom that had just been described.

The Lord used two figures of speech in 2:15 to describe the evils perpetrated by the Babylonians. On the one hand, they made their neighbors drunk; and on the other hand, they gazed shamelessly at their nakedness. As has been pointed out already, drunkenness was a particular sin of the Chaldeans. Not only did they drink to excess but they caused others to follow their bad example. As a consequence, a severe punishment would come upon them. They would be filled with disgrace rather than honor. Retribution would be in proportion to their sin (2:16*a*).

With verse 16*b*, there was a shift in emphasis. God entered the picture, as the metaphor changed slightly. "The cup in the Lord's right hand" (2:16*b*, NASB) would come around to the Chaldeans, and they would be required to drink of the "wine of the cup of His fury" (cf. Jer. 25:15, 17, 28; Obad. 1:16). Their former intemperance would turn into "utter disgrace" (2:16).

The Chaldeans had done more than debauch the nations they had conquered. They had stripped the land, denuded the forests (to provide cedar wood for the adornment of their own homes, buildings, and palaces), and destroyed the wildlife.

Only in comparatively recent years has the importance of conservation been understood. In the early chapters of Genesis, after God had made Adam and Eve and put them in the Garden to "tend and . . . keep it," He delegated to them and their descendants the responsibility to rule the earth on His behalf (Gen. 2:15, *The Amplified Bible;* Gen. 1:26-28). As a consequence of sin entering into the world, mankind became self-centered rather than God-centered. Men abused the provisions God had made for their enjoyment and systematically destroyed the earth's resources merely to have what they wanted. As a consequence, the land lost its strength, and the air and water their purity. Belatedly people are realizing that they must accept responsibility for natural resources they once took for granted. Just as God called the Chaldeans to account for their abuse of His creation, so He indictes men today for their wanton destruction of the earth's natural resources.

(5) For Their Idolatry, 2:18-19

The taunt song taken up against the Chaldeans shifted its focus in 2:18. The fifth woe (2:18-19), introduced by that verse, brought to the fore yet another sin. It was idolatry. The taunt was taken up against the makers of idols and the practice of sorcery (cf. Dan. 2:2, 4-5; 3:4-12; 4:7).

It is axiomatic that a people become like the things they worship. Whereas the gods of the Babylonians were cruel and licentious, they were also impotent. As a result, when the day of reckoning came, they were unable to protect those who had placed their trust in them.

Although some have believed that either by ventriloquism or perhaps through satanic power the Babylonian idols were made to "speak," the fact remains that the idols were without power or wisdom. They could neither help nor instruct. As beautiful as they might have appeared when overlaid with gold or silver, they were nonetheless lifeless.

Habakkuk derided those who worshiped such idols and called upon them to "Awake" and to "Arise" (NASB). Their cries only called attention to the impotence of the things they venerated.

Some who read Habakkuk's prophecy may think that it had application only to a time and people who lived thousands of years ago. The facts show otherwise. It is estimated that in the United Kingdom today there are more witches and warlocks than there are ministers of the gospel. In the United States as well there has been an immense increase in Satanism, theosophy, astrology, and the practice of occultism.

The appeal today of perverse and demonic worship should not be surprising, for when the apostle Paul wrote to Timothy (1 Tim. 4:1ff.), he stated that in the last days some would depart "from the faith, paying attention to deceitful spirits and doctrines of demons" (1 Tim. 4:1, NASB). Today his prediction is being fulfilled.

Lest men should lose heart, however, the proclamation of woes in Habakkuk's prophecy concluded with an important word of encouragement. God was in His Temple. He was still sovereign. He orchestrated the affairs of men to serve His purpose. There was blessing for those who placed their trust in Him.

3. GOD'S HOLINESS VINDICATED, 2:20

In spite of all that had gone on, Habakkuk wrote with certainty that the Lord was not powerless. He was not like the idols the pagans thought would bring health, wealth, and eternal life. He was worthy of praise, worship, and adoration:

> But the LORD is in His holy Temple.
> Let all the earth be silent before Him.
> (2:20, NASB)

As with Isaiah, who saw the Lord "high and lifted up" (Isa. 6:1-3, KJV), so in Habakkuk those on earth were bidden to contemplate Him (cf. Ps. 46:10) and to bow in reverential awe before Him.

Much has taken place in the history since Habakkuk's time, but God has not lost control of the events. Let the earth be quiet before Him.

As Habakkuk concluded the vision God had given him, he sensed inwardly God's holiness, righteousness, and justice. While His ways were not the ways of men, nor His thoughts the thoughts of men (Isa. 55:8-9), what the Lord chose to show to the prophet fully vindicated His wisdom and holiness. Habakkuk was left with a vision of God's glory and was brought to a position of implicit trust (cf. 2:4c). All of that led him to prepare a prayer of praise in honor of the Lord—a prayer that, in all probability, Habakkuk planned to have sung by the Temple choir.

As one contemplates the momentous events that faced the children of Judah at the hands of the Chaldeans, it is well to remember that the just live by faith (2:4c). Faith is the key to unanswered prayer. It is grounded in the conviction that God hears and answers prayer and eventually will reward those who diligently seek Him. Faith is the key to triumphantly enduring suffering and oppression. It is established upon the belief that God will vindicate the righteous. Faith is the key to a correct view of history, for through faith the believer recognizes that God will work all things out according to the counsel of His perfect will.

Faith is the key to the problem of sin and the apparent triumph of evil. It is established upon the belief that God can make the wrath of men praise Him, that He will eventually judge wrongdoers for their sin, and that He will reward the upright in heart. And finally, faith is the key to sanity in the midst of adversity, for faith brings stability to a world of confusion, enabling men to trust when outward circumstances might otherwise bring them to the brink of despair.

4

II. THE PRAYER OF HABAKKUK, 3:1-19

Why do people suffer? Or more to the point, if God is holy and righteous and good, why does he allow suffering and evil to continue in the world? On every hand there are good people who are exploited or oppressed while the unrighteous seem to prosper. As Norman Anderson, the British jurist and lay theologian, has pointed out, it is virtually impossible to consider either the law of God or the love of God without reflecting upon the inevitability of human suffering.[1]

When confronted with the problems of theodicy, the late E. S. Brightman challenged the thinking of many. He pointed out that men have the idea that God is good. He reasoned, however, that if God was all-powerful (omnipotent) and all-loving (benevolent), He could remove evil and suffering from the earth. The fact that evil and suffering persist proves either that God was not all-powerful, or that He was not all-loving. Brightman was unwilling to part with a belief in God's benevolence and so concluded that God was limited in His person.[2] The passage of Habakkuk under consideration in this chapter corrects the errors to which that kind of human reasoning leads.

As one wrestles with those themes, he is reminded again and again that calamity of one sort or another has overtaken him, someone he knows, or someone he has read about or has seen on the news. It is hard for him to reconcile the presence of such misery with the existence of an omnipotent, loving God.

The polytheist sees the world as dominated by gods and

---

1. J. N. D. Anderson, *God's Law and God's Love* (London: Collins, 1980), pp. 135ff.
2. E. S. Brightman, *The Problem of God* (New York: Abingdon, 1930), pp. 96-98.

spirits, both good and evil, who coexist. The former are beneficient, the latter, malignant. If he keeps on good terms with the
beneficient deities and spirits, all will be well. If he offends one
of the malignant forces, then evil will befall him. His duty is to
placate the latter gods and earn the favor of the former.

The pantheist sees Nature as being kind or cruel, tranquil or
stormy, depending on the situation. By depersonalizing God,
the pantheist removes himself from the position of believing
that he must defend Him. The variegated experiences of life are
accepted, therefore, without theological concern.

The dualist adheres to the belief that two co-eternal principles exist. The one is wholly good and the other is wholly evil.

Dualism finds divergent expression in Hinduism and Buddhism. Interestingly, in spite of their dualism both Hinduism
and Buddhism have become exceedingly complex systems in
the centuries they have existed. Basically, both groups view suffering as inevitable. They force a dichotomy between the body
and the spirit, believing that the inner faculty of man grows until it lays aside the impermanent (i.e., the body and the world)
and assumes the permanent (the final deliverance of the spirit).
At that time, all suffering is believed to cease.[3]

As one considers Christianity, he can observe in the Lord
Jesus One who looked at suffering with clear eyes and calm
confidence. He saw no reason to reject, refuse, or eliminate the
cross. To be sure, He knew the horror of His approaching
death (Matt. 26:38, 39; Heb. 5:7) and drank to the dregs the
cup of sorrow that His Father had given Him (cf. Matt.
20:22-23; Isa. 53:3-5, 10-12). And having suffered, He is able
to come to the aid of those who are afflicted (cf. Heb. 2:18).[4]

Inasmuch as Christ has suffered, His disciples should not
shrink from sharing that experience. The Scriptures even encourage the believer with the thought that suffering is one of
the means God uses to further his growth and bring him to

3. For a full discussion of the ways in which different religious beliefs approach the problem of suffering, see J. Bowker, *Problems of Suffering in
the Religions of the World* (Cambridge: Cambridge U., 1970).
4. Stephen Neill, *Christian Faith and Other Faiths* (London: Oxford U.,
1961), p. 123.

greater personal maturity (cf. Heb. 12:2-6; James 1:2-4). Suffering may be corrective also (cf. Gal. 6:7), and in such instances should be viewed as a discipline rather than a form of punishment. At other times, a person may bear hurts inflicted upon him solely on account of the malice of others. His response should be to draw closer to the Lord (cf. Rom. 8:18), knowing that Christ Himself, though sinless, was made perfect through the things He suffered (Heb. 2:10; 5:8). As a consequence, He can identify with the sufferings of men and can provide "grace to help in time of need" (Heb. 4:15-16). Then those He has aided may reach out and help others who are enduring times of adversity or affliction (2 Cor. 1:3-7).

To the believer, therefore, suffering is not only something to be viewed theologically, but is also something to be appreciated for its practical ramifications. In the final analysis, what Habakkuk revealed remains true today: "The righteous will live by his faith" (Hab. 2:4*c,* NASB).

A. Prayer for God's Future Intervention, 3:1-2

The prayer of Habakkuk is one of the finest Hebrew poems in the entire Old Testament. It was written in the form of a psalm and was probably designed to be sung by Levites in the Temple services (1 Chron. 25:1-8).

There are those who, with Pusey,[5] believe that only verse 2 of chapter 3 can properly be regarded as a prayer. Yet careful study leads to the conclusion that verse 1 of the chapter is a summary statement (or caption heading) relating to all that follows. It is preferable, therefore, instead of defining prayer in terms of limited, preconceived notions, to enlarge one's concept of prayer to include the kind of outpouring of the human heart so dramatically brought before the reader in this chapter of Habakkuk.

Although higher criticism has commonly denied that the psalm came from the pen of God's prophet, there is no compelling reason to deny that Habakkuk wrote it. Viewed in light of the context, it becomes the capstone of the book and reveals

5. E. B. Pusey, *The Minor Prophets* (Grand Rapids: Baker, 1953), 2:204.

the triumph of faith in the face of adversity. It is a fitting conclusion to the theme of the book. As such, it records a touching and heartwarming example of the manner in which the just can triumph over the adversities of life. Habakkuk looked beyond the vicissitudes of daily life and the threat of invasion to a time when God would right the wrongs of mankind and reward His servants for their faithfulness.

The prayer was designed to be set to music. The expression of 3:1, *Shigionoth,* the plural of *shiggaion,* may have referred to a passionate, emotional hymn or to some form of musical instrument. More likely it was the former.

The prophet presented his petition in 3:2. It was limited to that verse and was answered in 3:3-15. Then, in 3:16-19, Habakkuk recorded his response to 3:3-15. As was mentioned earlier, the concept of prayer many persons have needs to be enlarged to include the content of this chapter. What the Lord had earlier revealed to Habakkuk gave rise to this psalm of hope. Furthermore, what lies latent in Habakkuk's words in 3:16-19 may well be considered as a plea for future deliverance and a celebration of God's goodness.

In 3:2 Habakkuk responded to the vision God had given him in the earlier portion of the prophecy. He had been granted a preview of the punishment to come upon Judah and the retributive justice to be meted out to the Chaldeans. What he had heard and seen filled him with fear. His fear was not a neurotic apprehension but rather was reverential awe of God. God had condescended to take him into His counsels, and Habakkuk was overcome with wonder at the magnitude of what the Lord had revealed to him.

Revivalist preachers have often used 3:2 as a basis for stirring the emotions of God's people. What Habakkuk probably had in mind, however, was an appeal to the Lord to revive His work (i.e., to renew His deeds) in that day so that grace would be extended to God's people and they would be preserved through the coming judgment. That is why he entreated the Lord "in the midst of the years" to "make [His work] known" (NASB). He was concerned about the spiritual state of God's people and desired them to be spiritually ready for the trouble that was soon to come. Judgment was inevitable. But God might "in wrath remember mercy" for a people who were walking with Him and were living in obedience to His Word.

As Habakkuk reflected upon God's past dealings with Israel, he recalled an instance in which God's people were delivered from oppression when He heard their prayers and intervened on their behalf. Habakkuk's recollection was of the Exodus, particularly the entrance of the Israelites into the Promised Land, and in 3:3-15 the prophet gave a poignant description of the events that took place at that time.

B. PRAISE FOR GOD'S PAST INTERVENTION, 3:3-15

Although many modern scholars try to play down the significance of the Exodus,[6] the fact remains that throughout biblical history, the event was looked upon as a great one.[7]

When the reader assesses the middle portion of Habakkuk's prayer, he immediately encounters a phenomenon commonly seen in apocalyptic literature. The past seems to be linked with the future in ways that puzzle the Occidental mind. On the one hand, there appears to be a clear reference to what God wrought when He delivered the Israelites from Egypt; and on the other, there seems to be a foreshadowing of some future deliverance. Those two aspects need to be kept in mind in considering what God revealed to Habakkuk.

A second problem that faces the reader concerns the interpretation of such expressions as "God comes from Teman. . . . His splendor covers the heavens" (3:3, NASB); "He has rays flashing forth from His hand, and there is no hiding from His power" (3:4); "He stood and surveyed the earth; He looked and startled the nations. Yes, the perpetual mountains were shattered, the ancient hills collapsed. . . . I saw the tents of Cushan under distress, the tent curtains of the land of Midian were trembling" (3:6-7, NASB).

6. Cf. J. A. Wilson, *The Burden of Egypt* (Chicago: U. of Chicago, 1965), pp. 255-56.
7. Cf. Ex. 10:2; 13:3, 8-9, 14; Num. 15:41; 20:16; Deut. 4:34, 37; 5:6; 6:12-13, 21; 11:3-4; Josh. 24:6-7, 14, 17; Judg. 2:1, 12; 1 Sam. 10:18; 12:8; 2 Sam. 7:23; 1 Kings 8:16, 51, 53.

A look at a map of the ancient Near East will quickly show how far apart those places are. What happened to cause a disturbance in all of them? Also, though it is possible to explain the expressions as poetic imagery, a belief in the literal interpretation of Scripture necessitates holding the view that behind each figure of speech lies a literal reality. What was that literal reality?

It may be helpful, therefore, to consider a *possible* solution to these descriptive terms before examining what the text has to say about God's person (3:3-4) and power (3:5-15). No believer in the Bible doubts the miraculous intervention of God in the deliverance of His ancient people Israel from slavery in Egypt. In miraculous ways He set them free. In doing so, He crushed the might of Pharaoh, the most powerful monarch of that day. He parted the Red Sea and also divided the waters when the Israelites crossed the River Jordan (Josh. 3:14-17).

At times, God uses natural means, and at other times, He does not. Bible scholars are now reasonably sure that when the Israelites crossed the River Jordan a section of the bank collapsed, causing the water to mount up on the one side while it receded on the other.[8] Such an explanation does not eliminate the miraculous; rather, it enhances it, for whatever means God used, the waters parted as soon as the feet of the priests reached the bank of the river.

Three words—*môpēt, niplā'ôt,* and *ṭemāh*—are used in the Old Testament to describe the activity of God in nature and history. The words are variously translated "signs," "wonders" (cf. Ex. 7:3; Deut. 4:34; both NASB), "mighty acts" or "great works" (cf. Deut. 11:3, 7), and "power(s)" (cf. Ex. 32:11). Inasmuch as each of these words was used to describe some facet of God's activity in delivering His people from bondage in Egypt, it is unwise for a person to limit Him by imposing his own idea of the miraculous upon the events.

8. Cf. J. B. Free, *Archeology and Bible History* (Wheaton: Scripture Press, 1962), 128-29; E. B. Smick, *Archeology of the Jordan Valley* (Grand Rapids: Baker, 1973), pp. 61-63; M. F. Unger, *Unger's Commentary on the Old Testament,* 1:287. Free holds to the possibility that a volcanic eruption caused the banks of the Jordan to collapse at the precise time the Israelites were getting ready to cross the river.

Because the Exodus of the Israelites from Egypt has invariably been dated after 1445 B.C. (the biblical date according to 1 Kings 6:1),[9] some tacit evidence for a mid-fifteenth century date has been ignored by the majority of Bible scholars. A scholar who holds for an early date is professor Angelos Galanopoulos of the Athens Seismological Institute.[10] Galanopoulos has advanced a theory that may provide a basis for understanding that which Habakkuk saw. He believes that the volcanic eruption which destroyed a portion of the island of Santorini and almost all of the Mycenaean civilization may have been the cause under the guiding hand of God for some of the plagues of Egypt and the parting of the waters of the Red Sea.

After diligently examining and harmonizing ancient documents and following his own archeological excavations, Galanopoulos concluded that subterranean volcanic activity caused a deep-seated layer of pigment in the bed of the River Nile to turn the water to "blood" (Ex. 7:19-25, NASB), poisoning the fish and causing the frogs to seek sanctuary on land (Ex. 8:1-14). Then the eruption that caused the islands adjacent to Santorini to sink into the sea also caused volcanic ash to fall, bringing the plague of "murrain" on the cattle (Ex. 9:1-7, KJV) and perhaps even causing the boils that broke out on the people (Ex. 9:8-12).

The disturbance of the atmosphere was exceedingly great, much greater than that caused by the eruption of Mt. St. Helens. When Mount St. Helens exploded in Washington state on May 18, 1980, it initiated an avalanche of four billion yards of rock and ice, released with an explosive force of four hundred million tons of TNT, and leveled one hundred fifty square miles of prime forest. At Spirit Lake north of the volcano, an enormous water wave up to eight hundred fifty feet high

9. The Exodus is generally dated 1290 B.C. The conservative date, 1445 B.C. (the biblical date according to 1 Kings 6:1), has been ably defended by G. L. Archer, *Survey of the Old Testament Introduction* (Chicago: Moody, 1974), pp. 223-34.

10. Angelos G. Galanopoulos, *Seismikē geographia tēs Hellados* (Athens: Seismological Institute, 1955), and a work co-authored with Edward Bacon, *Atlantis: The Truth Behind the Legend* (London: Nelson, 1969).

stripped trees from the slopes of the adjacent hills. The eruption was infinitesimally smaller than the cataclysmic one of Santorini and the islands close to it. Thus the eruption at Santorini may well have brought about the unseasonable hail storm in Egypt (Ex. 9:17-35), and volcanic fallout from it could have caused darkness to cover the land (Ex. 10:21).

All of this reference to Santorini does not eliminate the miraculous from the biblical record. The fact that the plagues in Exodus were upon the Egyptians and that the Israelites living in the land of Goshen were spared highlights God's hand in the events. In addition, the miraculous is emphasized when it is realized that what God did in one section of the Mediterranean may have had an effect upon Egypt at the precise time Moses said it would.

Galanopoulos also believes that the gigantic tidal wave caused when the cone of the volcano on Santorini dropped into the sea may have brought about the phenomenon that enabled the Israelites to cross the "Sea of Reeds" (Heb., *yam suf;* translated "Red Sea" in the NASB and KJV). In the initial phase of the tidal wave the sea parted so that the Israelites escaped from Pharaoh's approaching army. The returning waters, however, completely covered the pursuing Egyptians and destroyed Pharaoh's army (Ex. 14:21-31).

Such a view helps to explain why Habakkuk saw in his vision the "tents of Cushan under distress, [and] the tent curtains of the land of Midian . . . trembling" (3:7, NASB). It may also serve to account for God's "rage against the rivers . . . [and] wrath against the sea," (3:8, NASB) in which God is described as a military Conqueror riding on His horses while bringing salvation to His people.

Such a view helps explain as well Habakkuk's statement that the Lord's "bow was made bare [and] the rods of chastisement were sworn. [He divided] the earth. . . . The mountains saw [Him] and quaked" (3:9-10*a,* NASB). The waters poured into the open crater made when the mountain split, and "the deep uttered forth its voice, it lifted high its hands" (3:10*b*)—a possible allusion to the sudden rising of steam caused by the in-rushing sea merging with the volcanic lava. Upon rising into the atmosphere, cooling, and being driven by a strong east wind (cf. Ex. 14:21), the steam could easily have resulted in hail upon the land of Egypt.

Whether one accepts that possibility or not, a consideration of it does give background for an evaluation of what God has chosen to reveal in the Bible.[11] Whatever the means God used when He caused "signs and wonders" in Egypt, the events of the Exodus were miraculous. Habakkuk saw those events from a heavenly perspective.

1. PRAISE FOR GOD'S PERSON, 3:3-4

Habakkuk wrote as if he were present at the time of the Exodus. The imagery he used to describe what he saw was vivid and dramatic. As Frank Gaebelein shows, "There is more behind the words [of Habakkuk] than natural catastrophes."[12] The theophany that God gave His prophet linked the past with the future and served to assure His people that just as He manifested His power in redeeming them out of Egypt and in judging Pharaoh, so He would again deliver the remnant of His people and judge their enemies.

In his prayer Habakkuk portrayed God as coming "from Teman," a district of Edom, and from Mt. Paran, a region south of Seir. Habakkuk amplified the word he used for God, *'Eloah,* by the descriptive term "Holy One," emphasizing a specific aspect of God's deity in keeping with the judgment He was about to execute. The historic backdrop of the events described by Habakkuk were portrayed by Isaiah as having a future fulfillment. Isaiah described the Lord as advancing in judgment upon his enemies and coming "from Edom with dyed garments from Bozrah" (Isa. 63:1-6). The context of Isaiah's prophecy definitely has application to the second advent of Christ and the events bringing to a close the Battle of Armaggedon. That which Habakkuk saw, therefore, apparent-

11. The late Alva J. McClain in *The Greatness of the Kingdom* (Chicago: Moody, 1959), pp. 28-36, draws attention to passages of Scripture such as Deut. 4:34-35; Ps. 135:6-9; 148:8; and Dan. 6:27 and makes astute remarks concerning God's activity behind the phenomena that are observable to the natural eye.

12. F. E. Gaebelein, *Four Minor Prophets* (Chicago: Moody, 1970), p. 182.

ly had more than one fulfillment. It had an immediate context that foreshadowed a final, ultimate victory.

It is fitting that, following such a description of the Lord, there should have been a pause. The prophet inserted the word "Selah" in the text, apparently for the purpose of giving worshipers time to pause and reflect upon the truth that had just been expressed. There are those who believe that in keeping with Habakkuk's position in the Temple choir, the word "Selah" gave instruction to the choir director to insert a musical interlude while the worshipers had time for reflection. Habakkuk used the word in verses 9 and 13 also. Its appearance in the chapter was unique, for apart from appearance in Habakkuk, it can be seen elsewhere in the Bible only in Psalms.

As Habakkuk continued his portrayal of God's Person, he viewed from a heavenly perspective that which God had wrought for the Israelites centuries before. God's glory covered the heavens and His splendor incited those on earth to praise Him. The Israelites saw the evidence of God's presence with them in the "pillar of cloud" by day and the "pillar of fire" by night (Ex. 13:21, NASB), and they sang praises to God following their deliverance. Their experience, Habakkuk asserted in 3:3 (cf. 2:14), foreshadowed a day to come when God's splendor would be openly manifested and He would be accorded universal adoration. The complete fulfillment of the events in Exodus would come at the inauguration of His kingdom.

Having introduced the thought of the effulgence of God's glory (cf. Heb. 1:1-3), Habakkuk then described the moral perfection of His Person and the power (symbolized in the King James by the word "horns") He wields. In poetic imagery, Habakkuk spoke of rays of light "flashing from His hands" (3:4, NASB), symbolizing the moral perfection of His character and the authority with which He metes out justice. Yet even in the revelation God gave of His Person, there was the "hiding of His power," for no human being can look upon the unveiled, infinite glory of God and live (3:4, NASB; cf. Ex. 33:20).

It is no wonder, therefore, that with such a vision of the inef-

fable majesty of God in his mind, Habakkuk was moved to
praise. There is nothing that more befits the creature when in
the presence of his Creator, or the believer in contemplation of
his Redeemer.

2. PRAISE FOR GOD'S POWER, 3:5-15

After having been given a vivid picture of the glory and
power of God, Habakkuk then saw in kaleidoscopic brevity the
judgments of God upon those who opposed Him (cf. Ex.
12:29-30). As Tatford points out, Habakkuk pictured Jehovah
"as riding on the storm and, like a victorious Ruler, making
His triumphal procession through the countries of His foes."[13]
In considering the latter part of 3:6, Tatford notes that the
storm described by Habakkuk was apparently accompanied by
an earthquake of considerable proportions. The earth was
shaken, the primeval mountains crumbled, the hills sank down
to the level of the plains, and the desert tribes recoiled in terror
at the natural phenomenon that had overtaken them so suddenly.[14]

Unger draws attention to the prophetic retrospect and prospect of the verses. In them he sees God "dealing with His elect,
covenant people," and, he observes, "in His planned purpose
for them in His chastening of them and His punishment of the
wicked," there is evidence that His ways are "everlasting."[15]
In much the same way God worked on behalf of Israel at the
time of the Exodus, so He shall work on behalf of His people
in the future to deliver them from all who oppress them.

As has been mentioned previously, Habakkuk spoke of the
far-reaching effects of that which took place at the time of the
Exodus. Nations far removed from Egypt were "startled"
(NASB) by unusually strong winds. Those winds distressed the

13. F. A. Tatford, *Prophet of the Watchtower: An Exposition of Habakkuk*
    vol. 2 of *The Minor Prophets* (Minneapolis: Klock and Klock, 1983),
    54-55; cf. S. R. Driver, *The Minor Prophets,* The Century Bible (Edin-
    burgh: T. C. and E. C. Black, 1960), pp. 82-89.
14. Tatford, *Prophet of the Watchtower,* p. 55. C. F. Keil, *Bible Com-
    mentary on the Old Testament: The Minor Prophets* (Grand Rapids:
    Eerdmans, n.d.), 2:102, is in essential agreement with this view.
15. Unger, *Unger's Commentary on the Old Testament,* 2:1912.

tents of Cushan and ripped at the tent curtains of those living in the land of Midian (3:7, NASB; cf. Ex. 15:14-16).

In continuing his revelation of the power of God, Habakkuk described both God's wrath and His mercy (3:8-15). Habakkuk shifted the scene from the tents of Cushan and Midian to the rivers and the sea. In poetic form, the prophet addressed the Lord in a series of rhetorical questions. In Hebrew thought, the negative form implies an affirmative statement. Although it is possible to see in the mention of "the rivers" a reference to the River Nile and perhaps to the River Jordan (Josh. 3:16), and to see in the mention of God's "anger against the sea" (3:8; Ex. 14:16, 21; Ps. 114:3, 5) an oblique reference to the Red Sea, the events may be more far-reaching in their scope (Ex. 14:21-22). What Habakkuk vividly portrayed was God as a Warrior riding upon His horses (cf. Deut. 33:26; Ps. 18:10) and marshaling His army (symbolized by His chariots, Ps. 68:17; Isa. 19:1) so as to bring salvation to His people.

Far from being displeased with the rivers or angry against the sea, the Lord, in revealing His power, intimated His willingness to intervene on behalf of His people. Thus by making His "bow" ready and preparing His "rods" to chasten the unrepentant, He demonstrated the freedom of His actions as well as the righteousness of that which He was about to do. Unger correctly points out that "the LORD's miraculous interventions on behalf of the covenant people were not confined to one period, but . . . His promsies, sealed by His oaths to His people, were a guarantee" of His continued intervention.[16]

Once again "Selah" is inserted into the text. Time was given God's people for mature introspection and a consideration of all that He had done for them. This was intended to give them hope as they faced the future (cf. Ps. 46:1-3; Jer. 30:5-7).

In fulfilling His promise to His people, the Lord was even prepared to "cleave the earth" (3:9, NASB; cf. Ezek. 38:20-22; 39:2-4; Rev. 16:1-21) and to cause the mountains to "quake" at His presence (3:10*a,* NASB; cf. Rev. 16:17-21). The sea ("the deep") would also be affected. It was described as both "utter[ing] forth its voice" and "lift[ing] high its hands"

16. Ibid., 1913.

(3:10*b*, NASB; a possible reference to steam).

In continuing the thought of God's leading His people out of Egypt and into the Promised Land, Habakkuk saw the sun and moon standing still in their places while God fought for Joshua against the Canaanites (3:11; Josh. 10:11-15; Ps. 18:9, 11). The reference to "the light of Thine arrows, at the radiance of Thy gleaming spear" (3:11, NASB) may have been a poetic way of describing the downward flight of the deadly hailstones that God sent upon the Canaanites and of the lightning that streaked the sky.

It is difficult to know what event Habakkuk had in mind in 3:12. The chronological sequence of events of the Exodus and entrance into Canaan seems to have been left behind, and what Habakkuk saw in 3:12 may have referred to Micah's prophecy (cf. Mic. 4:13) of the Almighty's trampling underfoot the nations of the earth (cf. Ps. 68:7; Isa. 63:1-3; Rev. 19:15-19). If that is so, then what Habakkuk described was of great eschatological significance. He would have been looking far beyond his own time to the "end times" when rebellion against God by the Antichrist and his followers would reach its zenith (2 Thess. 2:4-12) and the Lord would return to earth with hot indignation to crush His enemies (cf. Rev. 14:14—15:1). Then, in judging the sins of those who lived upon the earth, He would "thresh" the nations whose time of judgment had come (3:12, KJV; cf. Isa. 41:15; Rev. 14:18-20). If the end times are in view in 3:12, the verse restates a theme seen elsewhere in the book: the judgment of the Chaldeans as foreshadowing a coming judgment upon all the nations.

In 3:13, Habakkuk gave a rationale for God's display of power and might. That which God chose to accomplish was for the "salvation of [His] people" (3:13*a*; cf. Ex. 15:2; and from a prophetic point of view, Zech. 12:4-9; 14:3-4; Matt. 24:29-31; Rev. 19:11—20:3). The events of 3:13, therefore, appear to describe that which God will do during the Tribulation (cf. Zech. 12:10—13:1), when He accomplishes the salvation of His people at the same time He strikes a deathblow at His adversaries (3:13*b*; cf. Rev. 13:1-17).

Again "Selah" appears in the text, calling upon worshipers to pause and reflect upon God's power and might. He is irresistable. The righteous may suffer and endure oppression, misunderstanding, and loss, but when He returns, God will exact to the full judgment upon His adversaries.

Habakkuk continued his description of the destruction of God's enemies in 3:14-15. The description brought to a fitting conclusion the theophany that God had given His prophet. Habakkuk portrayed the nations as mighty princes dressed in armor and prepared for combat (cf. Ps. 2). No opportunity would be given them to enter into a battle, however, for their weapons of destruction would be turned back upon themselves. Habakkuk pictured the Lord's adversaries as rushing in upon His people to destroy them. They had anticipated an easy victory, but would be utterly defeated. The tables would be turned against them, and their defeat would demonstrate that their confidence had been misplaced.

With that manifestation of power, power reminiscent of that He exercised at the time of the Exodus, the Lord would rout and destroy His enemies. Whether He would use natural forces in their destruction (cf. Judg. 5:20; 1 Sam. 7:10) was not stated by Habakkuk. Habakkuk's main thrust in chapter 3 was on God's judgment of the wicked for the wrongs they had inflicted upon His people, rather than on the means by which God would bring about that overthrow.

A reverent consideration of the teaching given in chapter 3 should bring confidence and encouragement to those who are downcast. Only in this life will believers have to suffer oppression wrongfully. Even though the forces of evil may seem stronger and more prevalent now than ever before in the history of mankind, God is unchanging, and He is at work behind the events that take place from day to day to bring to a fitting climax all that He purposed long ago. He knows how to deliver the righteous from adversity (cf. Pss. 7:1, 2; 17:13; 22:4-5, 8; 27:12; 31:1-2, 15; 33:18, 19) and will cause even the wrath of men to bring praise to His name.

5

II. THE PRAYER OF HABAKKUK,
3:1-19 (*CONTINUED*)

The vision which the Lord gave His prophet drew to a close in 3:15. The full impact of the momentous events that were to take place left Habakkuk shaken. The drama of the vision God had given him added weight and solemnity to the prophet's closing words. They were laden with emotion. In what he said, the reader can see the true heart of the man. He had come a long way spiritually since he first poured out his heart to the Lord and complained of His seeming inactivity in the face of the oppression and injustice so prevalent among His people.

In answering Habakkuk's prayer, the Lord had shown him the past. He had revealed to him His power in delivering His people from Egypt and leading them through the waters of the Jordan into the Promised Land. He had also shown Habakkuk the future. It would be a time of adversity, persecution, privation, and despair. Habakkuk, who had asked the Lord to revive His work "in the midst of the years" (3:2), came to demonstrate in his own person the faith that overcomes fear. He exemplified the man who has experienced the reality in his own life of the "revival" for which he had prayed.

As one compares the beginning of the book of Habakkuk with its closing, it is clear that outward circumstances had not changed. Only the prophet had changed. His former bewilderment and confusion had given way to peace and trust in the Lord. It was the Lord who then filled the prophet's vision and satisfied his soul. Although Habakkuk's questions had not been answered, his doubts had been resolved. The vision God had given him of His plan and purpose had met the deepest needs of his heart.

The same principle is true today. The closer we draw to the Lord, the more we become aware of His strength. In one of the darkest hours of the fledgling China Inland Mission, Hudson Taylor encouraged his discouraged colleagues with the words, "It doesn't matter really how great the pressure is, but only where the pressure lies." As adversity drives believers closer to Christ, they are able to see in Him the One who is sufficient for every need. He sustained Elijah in a time of deep discouragement (1 Kings 19:4-8) and Paul as he faced opposition in Corinth (Acts 18:9-11). He was a constant source of help and encouragement to many others of whom we read in Scripture (e.g., Heb. 11:32-40).

With those thoughts in mind, the reader is in a position to consider how Habakkuk saw himself following the vision the Lord had given him.

C. RESPONSE TO GOD'S FAITHFULNESS, 3:16-19

1. THE PROPHET'S CONCEPT OF HIMSELF, 3:16

The concluding paragraph gives a glimpse of the innermost working of the soul of the prophet. The theophany he had received left him deeply agitated. His innermost parts trembled with fear, his lips quivered, and his very bones seemed unable to support his body. Daniel was later to share the same type of experience (cf. Dan. 8:17-18, 27; 10:7-10, 15-19): awe before the vision God had given him.

Faith was his only ally. He knew there was nothing he could do but wait. Though from a human point of view the threat of the Chaldean invasion filled him with fear, he determined, in spite of that fear, to wait quietly for the day of trouble.

It is in Habakkuk's quiet waiting that some understanding of the dynamics of fear proves helpful. Fear arises in men's hearts when they attribute to a person, place, or thing two important characteristics: *almightiness* (the power to take away another's autonomy) and *impendency* (the power to do another harm). Those attributes properly belong to God.

Had Habakkuk looked solely at the threat of the Chaldean invasion, the prospect of suffering at their hands and perhaps even of being carried away into exile and sold into slavery would have proved too painful for him. By contrast, however, his faith sustained him. He placed himself unreservedly under

God's sovereign care and protection. In so doing he took the
anxiety out of the situation.

From Habakkuk's experience, we realize that an acknowl-
edgment of God's sovereignty is more than a topic of
theological discussion. It is an important fact. It has practical
relevance to everyone. As men relate to God, they become
secure. Believers are His children and therefore belong to Him.
He has redeemed them, and on that account they have worth.
He fills them with His Spirit, making them competent. By
means of His power, they are able to handle the difficult and
trying circumstances of life.

Habakkuk's faith and trust in the Lord illustrate the way
Christians today should face adversity. He did not give way to
fatalism, nor did he adopt a stoic attitude. He avoided the pit-
fall of passive resignation as well. Though his inward parts
trembled, his attitude was one of submission to the will of
God, and he exercised active dependence upon Him. The vision
he had seen had filled him with reverential awe and had lifted
him beyond the adverse circumstances that prevailed around
him. As Abraham had seen the Lord before leaving Chaldea
(Acts 7:24), so Habakkuk was given a vision of God's
greatness and glory before being taken to Chaldea.

2. THE PROPHET'S APPRAISAL OF THE SITUATION, 3:17

The vision of the Lord's ultimate triumph did not minimize
the awfulness of the judgment that awaited God's people.
Habakkuk was not blind to what the future held. He knew that
the invader would come and ruthlessly strip the land of all that
was worth taking. Davidson[1] prefers to translate the Hebrew
word *kî* in 3:17 as "for" rather than "though" and implies
that the tragedies Habakkuk described were the result of
natural causes. The majority of scholars, however, prefer to
see in the double triad of the verse the destruction, poverty,
and desolation that were to accompany Nebuchadnezzar's
hoards in their conquest of the land. The context of Habak-

1. A. B. Davidson, *The Books of Nahum, Habakkuk and Zephaniah,* Cambridge Bible for Schools and Colleges (Cambridge: Cambridge U., 1905),
p. 93. Cf. S. R. Driver, *The Minor Prophets,* The Century Bible (Edinburgh: T. C. and E. C. Black, 1960), p. 97.

kuk's prophecy fits such an interpretation.

Ironically, the land that flowed with milk and honey (Deut. 8:7-9; 11:9-15) was to become barren. The fruit tree, the olive tree, the vine, and the harvest field would yield nothing; the sheep would be plundered in the fold, and the cattle driven from their stalls (3:17). Everything that the people of Israel needed to sustain life would be taken from them. Their experience at the hands of invaders would be worse than anything their history had recorded.

3. THE PROPHET'S CONFIDENCE IN GOD, 3:18-19

In the closing verses of the book Habakkuk expressed his rejoicing (3:18) and his rest (3:19). While the description he had been given of the devastation of the land (3:17) intimated that every visible means of support would disappear, Habakkuk, nevertheless, stated emphaticaly, "Yet I will exhalt in the LORD, I will rejoice in the God of my salvation." His skepticism (cf. chap. 1) had been replaced by trust. The vision God had given him of His power sustained him.

a. The Prophet's Rejoicing, 3:18

As Habakkuk faced the future, he was filled with confidence. He knew that what was soon to take place would strip from Judah everything men regarded as having value. Yet in spite of outward circumstances, the Lord would be in control. In the light of His presence, the worthlessness of the transient things of life would become evident. The Lord was Habakkuk's joy and strength, his crown of glory, and his hope for the future. The prophet rejoiced, therefore, in his salvation. The reference in 3:18 was not solely to temporal salvation, but to eternal salvation as well. Though he lived more than six hundred years before Christ's advent, Habakkuk was assured of his personal ("my") salvation—as if it were already accomplished. In that connection, Laetsch points out that "the redemption of the Annointed is an eternal redemption, [and] retroactive in its effects"[2] (Rom. 4:1-25; Gal. 3:6-18; Heb. 9:12-15; 11:1-40).

Habakkuk relied upon the Lord for his eternal salvation,

2. T. Laetsch, *The Minor Prophets* (St. Louis: Concordia, 1956), p. 352.

and he realized that God would uphold him in all of the trials that were soon to come. The vision God had given Habakkuk of His activity behind the scenes had given the prophet confidence.

A similar awareness of God's goodness and grace toward them, and of His power and might, should likewise undergird Christians today as they face the troubles of life.

b. *The Prophet's Rest,* 3:19

Habakkuk's rejoicing was indicative of the attitude of his heart (3:19). It was one of worship. God was his strength. The demonstration of the power of the Almighty had filled Habakkuk's heart with confidence. The Lord had not explained everything to Habakkuk, nor had He answered all his questions, but He had shown Habakkuk something of His greatness, and that was sufficient. Habakkuk was content. He no longer questioned God's sovereign will. Instead, he willingly submitted himself to the will of God.

Such submission did not curtail Habakkuk's liberty or mortgage his freedom to the oppressive dictates of a despotic deity. It liberated him. He exclaimed, "God has made my feet like hind's feet," swift and sure. Instead of a slow faltering gait, characteristic of one whose life was lived in bondage, Habakkuk imagined instead the leap of a gazelle from one crag to another, sure of foot and demonstrating freedom.

The expression "upon my high places" (3:19; cf. Deut. 32:13; Ps. 18:33) described the hills surrounding the city of Jerusalem. Habakkuk did not hesitate to call them his own, possibly because he had abounding confidence in God and possibly because he realized that the Lord would one day restore Israel to the land. At that time the righteous dead of the Old Testament era would be resurrected to eternal life (Dan. 12:2) and would be given their inheritance. God would thus fulfill the promises He had made to Abraham (Gen. 12:1-3, cf. Heb. 11:13-16).

Habakkuk had ordered that his prophecy be set to music and sung to the accompaniment of stringed instruments (3:19*b*). As his great prayer-psalm drew to a conclusion and the music died away, those who first heard the prophecy could not have helped being affected by the note of confidence on which it ended. Regardless of his outward circumstances, the just would live by his faith (2:4). That which Habakkuk found true in his experience, still is true today. Believers can and should rejoice in the God of their salvation.

ZEPHANIAH

6

INTRODUCTION TO ZEPHANIAH

On a recent visit to the United Kingdom, my wife and I flew from Edinburgh, Scotland, to Belfast, Northern Ireland. Rain had been a daily part of our tour. On the morning of our departure, however, the clouds had disappeared and we were privileged to enjoy for a brief time the best weather Scotland affords.

When we were all aboard the twenty-passenger Loganair plane, the pilot's voice was heard over the intercom. He made the usual introductory remarks and then stated, "Because it is such a beautiful day, I have obtained permission for us to fly at 7,000 feet above sea level instead of the usual 17,000 feet. Visibility is between sixty and eighty miles. This should give you an excellent view of Scotland and also of the Irish Sea. Flying time will be about fifty minutes."

The plane rumbled down the airstrip and we were soon airborne. The vista below was breathtaking. The usual highways linking cities and villages north and south, east and west were clearly visible. So were the quaint little lanes that, to the traveler unfamiliar with the area, seem to lead nowhere in particular. Now it was plain that these winding roads led past farm houses to little villages and hamlets dotted across the countryside.

As we flew westward with the sun at our backs, the countryside appeared like a giant patchwork quilt of rich green with the borders of the irregular fields being marked off by hedges of a deeper hue. In addition, here and there were valleys too narrow and too steep for cultivation. In those valleys, trees and shrubs grew in profusion. Streams and lakes, so vital to irrigation, were also interspersed across the land. Farm houses with their little red roofs, white walls, and black painted beams appeared so beautiful that they would have done justice to any artist's canvas.

Occasionally, a field of gold gave to the patchwork of green a bit of added color. Those fields showed that the grain had been harvested and that the land was now ready for the plow.

Only those who have been privileged to enjoy such an experience will be able to sense the awe with which we gazed down upon this kaleidoscope of natural beauty.

The best, however, was yet to come. Suddenly, the pilot's voice broke in upon our reverie. "We are approaching Culzean [pronounced coo-leen] Castle. I am not supposed to do this, but I will bank the plane so that you can all get a good view." And there, hugging the jagged coastline opposite the Hebrides, was the kind of castle that would have inspired a dozen of Walt Disney's romantic tales. Its massive walls spoke eloquently of its resistance to attack, and its beautiful turrets and well-manicured courtyards bore mute testimony to a period long past when aesthetics was highly prized.

As I reflected on what we had been privileged to see, I could not help but ponder the relevance of it to the writings of Habakkuk and Zephaniah. On the one hand, we see them at the crossroads of God's purpose for His ancient people. Strands of prophetic truth run through their writings like highways linking cities which are miles apart. In addition, however, from a consideration of their lives and teaching, it is evident that the minutia in their writings has relevance, as well as purpose. It fills in the details that otherwise would pass by unnoticed, particularly when read by those who are only interested in the broad sweep of God's program for the ages.

Prophetic truth, however, was always forged on the anvil of human experience. It was portrayed by the writers against the backdrop of daily life and the events of the times. There was a time for plowing and a time for sowing, a time of waiting and a time for harvest. To many living away from the centers of commercial enterprise and political intrigue, the words of the prophets were ignored. Those people were left untouched by the power struggles between priests and princes. Eventually, however, they would be caught up in the events that had been predicted.

Interspersed through the prophetic writings was an emphasis on the kingdom. Like the Castle of Culzean on the rugged coastline of Ayrshire, Scotland, defying storms and the threat of invasion, so God's plan for the consummation of the age has withstood the opposition and defiance of those who have resisted His right to rule their lives. God's program centers in the coming of the Messiah, the Lord Jesus Christ, who, as Kings of kings and Lord of lords, will bring in a reign of everlasting righteousness.

I. AUTHOR AND DATE

Of Zephaniah virtually nothing is known beyond what he himself recorded in 1:1. His name means "Whom the LORD covers" or "Whom the LORD protects," and from that it has been deduced that he was born during the latter part of the reign of Manasseh (686-642 B.C.; cf. 2 Kings 21:16).

Contrary to the usual custom, Zephaniah traced his genealogy back to the fourth generation (contrast Jonah 1:1; Hos. 1:1; and Isa. 1:1, being the prophets who had preceded him, and Jer. 1:1, his contemporary). On that basis, Zephaniah laid claim to being the great-great-grandson of Hezekiah king of Judah (715-686 B.C.). Although he did not specifically add the words "the king" to the text, there seems little doubt that Zephaniah was hinting at his royal ancestry.

Although some scholars have sought to show the unlikelihood of Zephaniah's relation to King Hezekiah, it seems preferable to conclude with R. K. Harrison that Zephaniah was indeed of royal descent.[1] After examining the evidence, Charles Feinberg stated, "The arguments that have been advanced against this view are not convincing."[2]

Zephaniah specifically dated his ministry during the reign of Josiah (640-609 B.C.; cf. 2 Kings 22:1—23:30; 2 Chron. 34:1—35:24). The years of Josiah's reign were among the happiest in Judah's experience. They were characterized by peace, a measure of prosperity, and zealous reform. No out-

1. R. K. Harrison, *Introduction to the Old Testament* (Grand Rapids: Eerdmans, 1969), p. 939.
2. C. L. Feinberg, *The Minor Prophets* (Chicago: Moody, 1976), p. 221.

side enemies made war against Judah during that time, and the people could consolidate their position as the remnant of the Lord, following the deportation of Israel.

Josiah came to the throne at the tender age of eight. Religious idolatry was rampant because his father, Amon, had reverted to Manasseh's earlier evil practices. Josiah, however, had God-fearing advisors and they inclined his heart in the way of the Lord. At the age of sixteen "he began to seek after the God of David his father" (2 Chron. 34:3) and at the age of twenty he began to cleanse Jerusalem and Judah of the idolatrous objects that his father and grandfather had brought into the land (2 Chron. 34:3-7).

Based upon 1:1, Zephaniah's ministry could not have begun before 640 B.C., when Josiah began his reign. Because Zephaniah predicted Nineveh's overthrow in 612 B.C., he must have prophesied before that event, and, therefore, the end of his ministry could not have come later than 612 B.C.

Internal evidence is useful in establishing more specifically when the prophet ministered. The idolatrous practices of 1:4-6 parallel those spoken of in 2 Kings 23:4-14, and thus Zephaniah's prophecy may have been uttered shortly before Josiah began to purge Jerusalem and Judah in 628 B.C. (cf. 1:8-9, 12).[3]

On the other hand, from a historical point of view, Zephaniah's predictions could easily have been uttered between 624 and 620 B.C. and could have provided the impetus for the king's reforms.

However, there are evangelical Bible scholars of the caliber of C. L. Feinberg and F. A. Tatford who, on the basis of Jeremiah chapter 1 and in light of the reference to "the remnant of Baal" (1:4*b*), believe that Zephaniah's ministry followed Josiah's reform. They adhere to the belief that Josiah's

3. This is the view of most modern scholars, e.g., G. L. Archer, *Survey of the Old Testament Introduction* (Chicago: Moody, 1974), p. 354; B. S. Childs, *Introduction to the Old Testament as Scripture* (Philadelphia: Fortress, 1979), pp. 459-60; and O. Eissfeldt, *Einleitung in das Alten Testament* (Tübingen, W. Germany: J. C. B. Mohr, 1956), p. 520. For an extended discussion, see D. L. Williams, "The Date of Zephaniah," *Journal of Biblical Literature* 82 (1983): 77-88.

reform, although zealous, was outward and external and that Baal worship sprang up again in the hill country of Judah soon after the first wave of enthusiasm began to wear off. They also believe that it was not long before idolatry was openly practiced in Jerusalem. These conservative Semitic scholars are more inclined to place Zephaniah's prediction at about 615 B.C. They concur with H. A. Ironside that the object of the Holy Spirit seems to have been to warn the formalists of coming judgment, as well as to comfort the hearts of the godly remnant. The very fact that a remnant was distinguished from the rest of the people of Judah and Jerusalem implies that the latter were ripe for judgment; for were all going as it should, there would have been no occasion for the faithful to be thus distinguished.[4]

C. F. Keil, in his commentary on the Minor Prophets, also argues convincingly for a date after Josiah's reforms (c. 615 B.C.).[5]

II. HISTORICAL BACKGROUND

The late Harry Rimmer highlighted the importance of a thorough knowledge of the historical background in Bible study by referring to an incident that took place while he was a student at a college in California.

> The teacher of a course, Professor Rosenberger, was one of the ablest pedagogues who ever wasted her life in the more or less important task of teaching a rising generation how to think! At the end of the first few weeks in a class in English History, she informed the student group that the following day we would be privileged to have a test in this particular subject. When the class gathered for the happy event, there were twenty ques-

4. H. A. Ironside, *The Minor Prophets* (Neptune, N.J.: Loizeaux, 1976), p. 301.
5. *Bible Commentary on the Old Testament: The Minor Prophets* (Grand Rapids: Eerdmans, n.d.), 2:118-21; see also his *Manual of Historical-Critical Introduction to . . . the Old Testament* (Grand Rapids: Eerdmans, 1952), 1:416.

tions written on the board which were to constitute our examination.

The first question was something like this, "What new treaty had just been signed between France and Spain at this particular period?"

The next question had to do with the political commitments of the Holy Roman Empire.

The third question took us into the Germanic states, and in all of the twenty questions, not one word concerning England was mentioned!

As the class sat with the usual and habitual expression of vacuity which generally adorns the countenance of a college student facing a quiz, the Professor said, "You may begin."

Some hapless wight procured the courage to protest, by saying, "But you said this was to be an examination in English History!"

The Professor replied, "Quite so! This *is* English History!" Then leaning forward over the desk she said, in impressive tones, "How can you expect to know what England is doing, and why, if you do not know the pressure upon her of her enemies and friends at that particular period?"

A long distance back in our mental vacuum a dim light began to glow, and we never were caught that way again! . . . One day as we were thinking over this helpful technique of understanding, the idea began to grow that if this is the proper way to study secular history, *it ought to apply to Bible study as well!*

There is an illumination that brightens the meaning of the Sacred Text when read in the light of collateral events that can come in no other way.[6]

The book of Zephaniah must be viewed against a threefold background:

6. H. Rimmer, *Dead Men Tell Tales* (Grand Rapids: Eerdmans, 1945), pp. 15-17.

(1) Assyrian supremacy;
(2) The Scythian invasion; and
(3) Independent power struggles preceding the emergence of the Neo-Babylonian empire.

A. THE ASSYRIANS

Prior to the times of Josiah, in 721 B.C., the Assyrians, under Sargon II (722-705 B.C.), overran the ten northern tribes of Israel. The Assyrians, in deporting the people of Israel, resettled them in different places throughout the Tigris-Euphrates River valley and in Media (2 Kings 17:5-6). Residents from the upper classes of people in Babylonia and Syria were then settled in the cities of Samaria. This manner of mixing populations had been instituted by Tiglath-pileser III as a means of diminishing the chances of rebellion among subjugated peoples (2 Kings 17:24).

Those whom Sargon settled in Samaria were idolators. They intermarried with the Israelites who had been left behind by the Assyrians, and with intermarriage came also a religious syncretism, for the new settlers in Samaria brought with them their own pagan deities and manners of worship. The result was a repetition of the abuses that had brought about Israel's demise (2 Kings 17:29-41).

The merging of the Babylonian, Syrian, and Israelite races brought into being a new group known as Samaritans. Those in Judah looked with disdain upon their northern neighbors and had as little to do with them as possible (cf. John 4:9*b*).

Sargon had scarcely completed the overthrow of Israel when he was faced with rebellion in Babylonia. No sooner had this rebellion been put down when he became involved in other campaigns in Asia Minor and Urartu (ancient Armenia). When he died, he was followed on the throne successively by Sennacherib, Esarhaddon, and Ashurbanipal.

Sennacherib (705-681 B.C.) succeeded his father and likewise became involved in suppressing revolts within Assyria and as far west as Cilicia, where he captured the city of Tarsus in 698 B.C..

Sennacherib was murdered by one or more of his sons, and

Esarhaddon (680-669 B.C.) succeeded him. Esarhaddon, however, was faced with considerable opposition from peoples living to the north of Assyria, including the Cimmerians and Scythians. In the course of time, however, he invaded Egypt and, although his first attack failed, his second one in 672 B.C. was successful.

In attempting to consolidate his empire, Esarhaddon appointed Ashurbanipal (669-633 B.C.) as his successor. His death, however, interrupted his plans and it was left to Ashurbanipal to control and maintain his extensive domain.

Ashurbanipal's reign overlapped part of the reign of Josiah (640-609 B.C.). During his reign, Assyria relentlessly subjugated Egypt. Upon his death, however, the might of Assyria began to wane. Ashurbanipal's successors could do little to quell the forces arrayed against them. In 614 B.C. the Babylonians, aided by the Medes, overthrew the Assyrian capital of Asshur, and in 612 B.C. Nineveh suffered a similar fate.

B. THE SCYTHIANS

The Scythians were a nomadic people from the highlands of Asia who invaded the Mesopotamian Valley in the eighth century. They were known for their cruelty (see the Apocrypha, 2 Macc. 4:47; cf. 3 Macc. 7:5) and initially attacked the Assyrians along their northern frontiers in 632 B.C.[7] Their continued encroachments made it easy for Josiah, about a decade later, to engage in his reforms (cf. 2 Kings 23:15-23).

According to the Greek historian Herodotus (484-424 B.C.?), Scythian influence extended along the Palestinian coast to Egypt. Although some scholars doubt the veracity of Herodotus's report, modern researchers are finding increased confirmation of the general accuracy of his account.

Apparently, after marching down the coast, the Scythians reached the border of Egypt where Pharoah Psammetichus I (663-609 B.C.) protected his kingdom by buying them off.

---

7. Herodotus *History* 1. 104-6; H. H. Rowley, *Men of God: Studies in Old Testament History* (London: T. Nelson, 1963), p. 141; and J. P. Hyatt, "The Date and Background of Zephaniah," *Journal of Near Eastern Studies* 7 (1948): 25-29.

Those holding to a pre-620 B.C. date for Zephaniah's prophecy hold that the Scythian invasion was imminent and thus formed the background to the prophet's predictions. Such a view assumes that Judah was affected by their invasion—a view, however, which lacks definitive biblical and historical support.

C. INDEPENDENT POWER STRUGGLES

Although Judah enjoyed a period of political stability during the reign of Josiah, there was relatively little calm anywhere else. Of the two superpowers, Egypt was dominated by the Assyrians (under Esarhaddon and his son Ashurbanipal). When Assyria began to decline politically in the face of the increasing might of the Neo-Babylonian empire, the Egyptians fought two major battles against the Babylonians at Carchemish (modern Jerablus). They were nominally victorious in the first encounter (609 B.C. when Josiah was tragically killed, 2 Kings 23:29-30; 2 Chron. 35: 20-27; Jer. 46), but were severely beaten by Nebuchadnezzar in 605 B.C.

By his decisive victory, Nebuchadnezzar established Babylonian supremacy in the Near East. This turn of events was important for Israel, for it was the invasion by the Babylonians that Zephaniah predicted in 1:10-17; 2:4-7; and other passages.

III. THE THEME OF THE BOOK

Zephaniah is a book of synthesis designed to provide an overview of coming events. The modern era, however, is an age of analysis. As a consequence, readers today tend to approach the book from that perspective. The result is confusion, for Zephaniah's prophecy cannot be understood apart from an awareness of his theme and purpose. The reader must ask: What points did the prophet emphasize most? How did he develop his theme? When will the events he described take place?

The focus of the book of Zephaniah is on the "day of the Lord." The expression first appeared in Joel 1:15, and it had become popular among the people by the time of Amos (cf.

Amos 5:18-20). To those living in Old Testament times, the concept of the "day of the Lord" looked forward to the time when *Yahweh* would intervene in history on behalf of His chosen people, Israel. Israel would then become the head of the nations of the world and the channel of God's blessing to all people. Consequently, the theme of Zephaniah is laden with political overtones.

The concept of the "day of the Lord" that was popular initially was shown to be in error, however, for between the eighth and sixth centuries B.C. different prophets arose to correct the distorted view. They predicted that judgment would start with God's people, Israel (Isa. 2:5—3:26; Ezek. 13:5; Joel 1:15; 2:1, 11; Zeph. 1:7, 14; Zech. 14:1). They showed that the "day of the LORD" would begin with a battle cry (Ezek. 30:2-3; Isa. 13:6; Joel 1:15), as the Lord summoned His enemies to prepare for battle (Isa. 13:3-5). It would be a day of darkness (Ezek. 30:3) and fire (Zeph. 1:18; Mal. 4:1), and of cataclysmic events (Isa. 34:4) when those on earth would tremble (Joel 2:1-11). Babylon (Isa. 13:1, 6, 9), Egypt (Jer. 46:10-11), Edom (Obad. 1, 15), and the other nations (Joel 2:31; 3:14; Obad. 14) would be laid waste as God intervened to punish sin that had come to a climax.

The destruction of the earth would be as complete as the overthrow of Sodom and Gomorrah (Zeph. 2:9), and panic would seize old and young alike (Isa. 2:10, 19). They would hide themselves (Isa. 2:21; Rev. 6:15-16) in fear (Isa. 13:8) and confusion (Ezek. 7:7). Those unable to find shelter would stagger about like blind men (Zeph. 1:17) or else would be unable to stand upon their feet (Mal. 3:2). No one would have the heart to take up arms (Ezek. 7:17) or oppose God as He avenged Himself upon His enemies.

Zephaniah's description of this "day" of God's wrath was not immediately understood by those in Judah. Depending upon the time of his ministry and the uttering of those oracles, some of those who heard them may have thought that he was referring to the Scythians or the Assyrians. As is common in prophecy, Zephaniah blended the near and the far views of the

day of the Lord's intervention. In this connection, Gleason
Archer points out that there was a definite millennial overtone
to the promise in Zephaniah of the ultimate blessedness of
Israel (3:13).[8] The history of Zephaniah's times prefigured the
climactic events of the "end times."

In Zephaniah's prophecy, *Yahweh* is seen directing history
to its final outcome. The proclamation to Israel of a day of
judgment was also a proclamation of a day of reckoning for
the whole world. That "day" would not occur randomly but
would begin with the Tribulation period spoken of as the "time
of Jacob's trouble" (Jer. 30:7, KJV; cf. Isa. 24:20-21;
26:20-21; 34:1-3; Joel 1:15; 2:2; Amos 5:18; Zeph. 1:14-18; and
in the N.T., Rev. 6:16-17; 11:18; 14:19; 15:1, 7; 16:5-7; 19:1-2).

Originally, the "day of the LORD" was understood by the
people of Israel to imply God's judgment upon their enemies.
The prophets struggled against the false sense of security such a
view created. Those who thought they had a right to be
delivered unconditionally from all their troubles were not
prepared for a message in which the prophets, in announcing
Israel's involvement in the judgment of "that day," pointed
out that only a remnant would be saved (Isa. 28:14-22; Joel
1:15; Amos 5:18-20; Mic. 1:2-16).

In the New Testament, the coming of the Lord Jesus Christ
added a new dimension to the understanding of the "day of the
LORD." The event was seen as beginning with the Tribulation
period and embracing the whole of the Millennium. It was
spoken of by various writers as a "day of visitation" (1 Pet.
2:12), a "day of judgment" (2 Pet. 2:9), and a "day of wrath"
(Rev. 6:17).

The clearest picture in the Bible of the "day of the Lord"
was given by Zephaniah. Further elaboration upon that theme
will be undertaken in the exposition of the text. Before the text
can be properly expounded, however, consideration needs to
be given to certain critical problems affecting the unity of the
book.

8. Archer, p. 354.

IV. THE UNITY OF THE BOOK

Writers who have engaged in negative biblical criticism have invariably challenged the authenticity of certain sections of Zephaniah's prophecy. Although the majority have allowed chapter one to stand as a genuine work of the prophet, others have either seen in portions of Zephaniah the work of later editors or have claimed that chapters two and three were written after Zephaniah's death in the exilic or post-exilic periods.

For example, it is generally accepted by moderately liberal Bible critics that the prophetic sections of the Hebrew canon reached essentially their present formulation by 200 B.C., and that major alterations were not made after this point. It is also believed by some students of ancient historians that early writings do not record the exact words of an individual as the reader would demand of a modern record. They claim that the prophetic books demonstrate transmission-growth process. In such a process, the first major alteration was to expand the judgmental messages to Israel-Judah's enemies. The second major alteration, they believe, took place during the post-exilic era, when attention switched to a future age of restoration that would be accompanied by either the subjugation or conversion of the Gentiles. The process, it is held, is recognizable in the book of Zephaniah.[9] I cannot agree with such a view.

George Adam Smith, the Old Testament scholar from Aberdeen University of a generation ago, furnishes an interesting example of negative biblical criticism. He assumes that the text is faulty and therefore tries to correct it. The result is further confusion and disorder.[10]

R. K. Harrison provides a summary of the various aproaches to the authenticity of Zephaniah and shows how different writers who have dissected chapters 2 and 3 have arbitrarily assigned them to various time periods.[11]

The viewpoint of liberal critics is weak and based upon un-

9. *Broadman Bible Commentary,* ed. Clifton J. Allen et al., rev. ed. (Nashville: Broadman, 1972), 7:272.
10. G. A. Smith, *The Book of the Twelve Minor Prophets* (New York: Harper and Brothers, 1928), 2:35.
11. Harrison, pp. 941-42.

substantiated presuppositions. There is no valid evidence which would lead to the conclusion that Zephaniah did not write every word contained in the book that bears his name, or that what he wrote was not immediately recognized as the "word of the Lord" (1:1).

With confidence, therefore, the contents of Zephaniah may be surveyed and careful note taken of the nature and scope of its message.

V. Outline of the Book

I. Judgment of the Day of the Lord (1:1—3:8)
   Introduction (1:1)
   A. Judgment upon All the World (1:2-3)
   B. Judgment upon Judah (1:4—2:3)
      1. The Intent of the Judge (1:4-13)
         a. Judgment upon Religious Practices (1:4-6)
         b. Judgment upon Social Practices (1:7-13)
      2. Description of the Judgment (1:14-18)
         a. Its Imminence (1:14)
         b. Its Indignation (1:15-18)
      3. Purpose Behind the Warning (2:1-3)
   C. Judgment upon the Nations (2:4-15)
      1. Upon Philistia in the West (2:4-7)
      2. Upon Moab and Ammon in the East (2:8-11)
      3. Upon Ethiopia in the South (2:12)
      4. Upon Assyria in the North (2:13-15)
   D. Judgment upon Jerusalem (3:1-7)
      1. Summary of the Cause of Judgment (3:1-2)
      2. Specific People to Be Judged (3:3-4)
      3. Standard of Righteousness to Be Upheld (3:5)
      4. Stance of the People Toward the Warning (3:6-7)
   E. Judgment upon All Nations (3:8)
II. Salvation of the Day of the Lord (3:9-20)
   A. Conversion of the Nations (3:9)
   B. Restoration of Israel (3:10-20)
      1. Regathering of Israel (3:10)
      2. Redemption of Israel (3:11-13)
         a. Conversion of the Remnant (3:11-13*a*)
         b. Restoration of the Remnant (3:13*b*)
      3. Ruler over Israel (3:14-17)
         a. Rejoicing of the People (3:14-15*a*)
         b. Reign of the King (3:15*b*-17)
      4. Reward of Israel (3:18-20)

7

I. JUDGMENT OF THE DAY
OF THE LORD, 1:1—3:8

The thought that this world is ripening for the judgment of the "Day of the LORD" is scorned by some exponents of our culture. Alvin Toffler, for example, in *The Third Wave* has described the two prominent mindsets of most Westerners. Many people, he believes, are indifferent about the future. They are uniformitarian in their thinking. They presume that the world as they know it will last indefinitely. To them a different style of life is untenable.[1]

Toffler then analyzes the other group—those who, after reviewing the crises faced in every area of life, believe that there will not be a future, that man will destroy himself, that Armageddon is just around the corner.[2] Toffler blames such mass paranoia on the fact that people have been systematically brainwashed by the news, disaster movies, apocalyptic Bible stories, and nightmare scenarios. He and those writers who have expressed similar views scornfully repudiate all thought of divine intervention. Rather, they believe that there is a third view. They assert that we are at a "hinge" in history. The future presages a "giant transformation" in the way we live. A "global revolution" dominated by computers and technology is even now taking place. We constitute the final generation of the old order and the first generation of the new. What is even now becoming a reality will radically alter the way we live, but will in no way resemble what the Bible teaches.[3]

As valuable as the insights of these sociologists are, their work reflects a disdain for God's Word. In the thinking of such men, the prosaic writings of an inconspicuous Hebrew prophet

1. A. Toffler, *The Third Wave* (New York: William Morrow, 1980), p. 27.
2. Ibid., pp. 27-28.
3. Ibid., p. 28.

have no place. To those who value what God has chosen to reveal through His inspired penman, the prediction of Zephaniah, though difficult to understand, is nevertheless welcomed as the revelation of the Lord Himself.

To understand properly the "word of the Lord," it is necessary to travel back in time to the seventh century B.C. There we encounter a man who faithfully delivered God's message to God's people.

Who was he? What can we learn about him? Where did he live?

INTRODUCTION, 1:1

Because he lived in an age when names were bestowed upon children for special reasons, the name given Zephaniah was of particular importance. Its meaning, "whom the Lord hides," or "whom the Lord protects," seems to imply that Zephaniah had been born during the bloody and violent days of Manasseh (see Introduction).

Zephaniah specifically claimed to be a descendant of Hezekiah (728-686 B.C.; 2 Kings 20). Most commentators have accepted the conclusion of Aben Ezra that the Hezekiah referred to was indeed the king. If this was so, then Zephaniah was of royal blood.

Hezekiah's son, Manasseh, reigned for fifty-five years (2 Kings 21:1), and since Zephaniah prophesied after Josiah's reforms (about 615 B.C.), there was adequate time for the four generations mentioned in 1:1.

On the basis of 1:4, 10, 11, it has been assumed that Zephaniah was a resident of Jerusalem. Although this is probable, such a view cannot be confirmed.

Zephaniah ministered, however, in times much like the present. Josiah had been preceded by two evil kings, Manasseh and Amon. Their idolatry, witchcraft, and spiritism undid most of the good done earlier by Hezekiah (2 Chron. 32—33). The worship of the Baalim, the host of heaven (astral deities), and Molech had corrupted the land.

In the eighth year of his reign, however, Josiah had begun to seek the Lord. He removed from the land the altars and images of the false deities that the people had been worshiping. He also reinstituted the worship of *Yahweh* (2 Chron. 34:3-8). About ten years later, in 621 B.C., the book of Deuteronomy was found in the Temple. At the king's instigation, an even more intensive reform was inaugurated.

In the view of most conservative Bible scholars, the reformation begun by Josiah was neither complete nor entirely successful. Despite his attempts to put an end to the worship of Baal, a remnant of Baal-worshipers remained. Although images to the sun, moon, and stars were removed from the Temple of the Lord, these pagan deities were soon worshiped again openly on the rooftops of homes. Priests of the pagan idols, following the first flush of repentance, reappeared. Because there was no continuing suppression of idolatry, the people went on serving Baal and the Ashtaroth openly and without shame. Idol worship, therefore, remained woven into the everyday life of God's people.

By the time of Zephaniah, materialism had displaced spirituality, and in the pursuit of riches the wealthy were indulging in cruelty, injustice, and oppression. In the light of subsequent events, it would seem as though Josiah's reforms had touched only a small remnant of the people. The majority ably fitted Jeremiah's description of a nation ripe for judgment (cf. Jer. 1).

From that we learn an important lesson. The best endeavors and most ardent desires to serve the Lord will falter and fail if they bring about only an outward modification of a life-style with little internal change of heart.

A. JUDGMENT UPON ALL THE WORLD, 1:2-3

Zephaniah began his message with a harsh proclamation. He announced the inevitability and the extension of the Lord's judgment. Those who heard him might have expected him to declare judgment upon Judah's enemies, for that was the popular belief at the time (see Introduction). As will be seen, however, Zephaniah's words had both an immediate and a more distant application. The immediate or "near view" anticipated the coming Chaldean invasion. The more distant or "far view" saw the final outcome of those prophetic warnings as taking place in the Tribulation period.[4] Zephaniah began with a declaration of universal destruction. He gave no hope. God would consume and destroy everything on the face of the earth. The Hebrew text contains an alliterative device to emphasize the totality of God's judgment: "I will cut off mankind (*'Adam*) from the face of the earth ('Adamah)." Man and beast, bird and fish were to share a common fate.[5]

So extensive would that judgment be that obviously it would exceed anything Judah might have anticipated. Zephaniah presented the "day of the LORD" in its full scope. He carefully blended the near and the far prophetic views together and applied them to the impending judgment upon Judah from the Chaldeans. The immediate judgment of Judah prefigured a far greater worldwide time of trouble (Dan. 12:1; Matt. 24:21; Rev. 8:1—20:3) to come upon Israel and the nations of the world (Jer. 30:5-7; Joel 3:2-17). God's judgments in that time of trouble would be preparatory to Israel's final restoration and Kingdom blessing (Jer. 30:8-9; Joel 3:18-21; Amos 9:11-15; Zeph. 3:14-20; Hag. 2:20-23; Zech. 8:20-21; 14:16-21; Mal. 4:1-4; Acts 1:6; Rom. 11:25-36; Rev. 20:4-6). Thus while Zephaniah's prediction comprehended the coming invasion under Nebuchadnezzar, its language was far more comprehensive. From a careful reading of the text, it is clear that it "[embraced] the apocalyptic judgments of the Great Tribulation and the worldwide woe of that period," even while its immediate context was "designed to call out a saved remnant of the Jews" and leave the ungodly from both Israel and the nations to their fate.[6]

All of that Zephaniah made more specific in 1:30. There God stated that He was going to single out the wicked, for they had been stumbling blocks in the path of His people and had prevented or made impossible true allegiance to the Lord. The word *hammakhshēlôth*, "stumbling blocks" (translated

4. M. F. Unger, *Unger's Commentary on the OltTestament* (Chicago: Moody, 1981), 2:1923.

5. Ibid., pp.1923-24.

6. Ibid., p. 1923.

"wicked" in the NASB), reflected a nation brought to ruin by the sin of the people. The word comes from *makhshēlāh* and represents that against which, or through which, a person meets with a fall. The thought is of those objects of a coarser or more debasing idolatry through which the people had been caused to stumble. As a consequence, they had turned from the path of that which was right (cf. Isa. 3:8; Ezek. 14:3-4, 7).

On account of man's rebellion against God's rule, every moral, social, and political institution had become corrupt and thus had failed to fulfill the intention for which it had been instituted. For this reason God said in effect, "I will remove the cause of transgression from the face of the land."

The emphasis was unmistakable. The Hebrew text has an infinitive absolute, followed by two infinitive absolutes underscoring the severity of God's judgment. He was going to destroy all things utterly. The "coming Chaldean invasion of Judah by Nebuchadnezzar" was to be but the foreshadowing of the events of *the* "day of the Lord."[7] The culmination of God's plan would come in a satanically inspired human rebellion (Rev. 9:20-21; 16:13-16; 19:19; 20:1-3). The end of that period would witness the final and most fearful interposition of the Lord in history, for He was going to "destroy the wicked at the height of their rebellion" together with the Antichrist and the false prophet (Rev. 13:1—16:21).[8]

B. JUDGMENT UPON JUDAH, 1:4—2:3

In his opening comments, Zephaniah addressed the nations of the world in general. He then became more specific and turned his attention upon Judah. Scripture teaches that judgment always begins with the "household of God" (1 Pet. 4:17). It should not be surprising, therefore, that the prophet turned from a general denunciation of evil to single out specifically those in Judah whose privileges should have made them a light to the Gentiles.

As the content of the verses is considered, it will be useful to

7. Ibid.
8. Ibid., p. 1924.

keep in mind that Zephaniah's prophecy ultimately looked at *the* coming "day of the Lord." Because that prediction was uttered at a time in which it also anticipated the coming Chaldean invasion, Zephaniah's words may also be applied to *a* "day of the Lord" in which God's hand would be stretched out against Judah and Jerusalem.[9] He was going to intervene in history to punish the sins of His people. The pending judgment at the hands of the Babylonians (i.e., Chaldeans) was to be illustrative of what would take place on a worldwide scale at the end of the age.

The consistency of such a view of Zephaniah's prophecy may be seen in his reference to "the remnant" (1:4, NASB) and in his saying that judgment was to come upon "the rulers, and the king's sons" (1:8), rather than his singling out the sons of Josiah by name. As a remnant would be kept safe during the coming Chaldean invasion, so Israel would be preserved through the Tribulation period.

1. THE INTENT OF THE JUDGE, 1:4-13

God's words through His prophet were as harsh as they were unexpected (1:4). It would have been easy for those living in Jerusalem to understand the anger of the Lord against the Gentile nations. Certainly their evils would have demanded just judicial action. The Israelites, however, were ill prepared for such an indictment of their own lives and religious practices. After all, had they not just come through a period of vigorous reform?

a. Judgment on Religious Practices, 1:4-6

It is easy for those who study Zephaniah today to lose sight of the fact that God's people had been blessed above all other nations. Their base ingratitude to Him and numerous breaches of the covenant relationship were ample cause to bring down His wrath upon them. They boasted arrogantly of their relationship to God and yet turned their backs upon His service, bowed down before Baal, and worshiped the "host of heaven"

9. Ibid., p. 1923.

upon the rooftops of their houses. Inasmuch as their wickedness had come up before the face of the Lord (Matt. 1:7), so now He was about to recompense them for their deeds. He intended to remove the "remnant of Baal" from the land.

In the Canaanite pantheon, Baal was the son of El. He was the god of fertility as well as the god of the storm and of war. His worship was extremely sensual. Open immorality was practiced "on every high hill" and "under every green tree" (1 Kings 14:23). Baal's sister-consort was Anat, sometimes referred to as Anath. Her characteristics complemented his. Religious or "sacred" prostitution was practiced in her name by the priestesses connected with her temples. All of that was done to ensure the fertility of the earth and an abundant harvest. It was believed that if Baal and Anat saw humans cohabiting on earth, they would be reminded of their own conjugal responsibilities. Their cosmic union would then produce on earth bountiful crops and increase the size of flocks and herds.

From 1 Kings 18—19, it is known that Baal-worship was conducted by persons especially consecrated to the task. The priests of Baal, together with those who followed them, were now to come under the rod of God's anger. Zephaniah spoke of them as *kemârîm*, "idolaters," and not as prophets per se (cf. 2 Kings 23:5 and Hosea 10:5). Initially they had been appointed priests by the kings of Judah for the purpose of leading people in worship of God. But the *kōhănîm* ("priests," cf. 1 Kings 12:31, 32; 13:33), it appears, had become idolaters and had apostatized from the Lord. They had forfeited their right to be priests of God. Now, together with those who followed them, they were to be cut off.[10]

Having delivered his initial general indictment, Zephaniah then became even more specific. Judgment was to fall upon men and women—in fact upon all who at sunset bowed down to the "host of heaven" upon the roofs of their houses (1:5).

F. A. Tatford observes that from early days of human

10. C. F. Keil, "Zephaniah," *Bible Commentary on the Old Testament: The Minor Prophets* (Grand Rapids: Eerdmans, n.d.), 2:128

history, the sun, moon, and stars have been worshiped.[11] In
Egyptian, Sumerian, and Akkadian religion, the sun was re-
garded as a deity, and there were certainly sun worshipers in
Babylonia and Assyria. Sabaism (the worship of the stars) was
also practiced widely among the Semitic peoples. Manasseh not
only introduced astral worship into Jerusalem, he also set up
altars to the astral deities in the temple of Jehovah, which
Josiah subsequently destroyed (2 Kings 21:3-5; 23:4-5).
Jeremiah implied that such worship was almost universal in
Jerusalem (Jer. 19:13).

In 1:6, the prophet highlights God's intimate knowledge of
the condition of His people. He indicted two specific classes of
people. First, were those who had known the truth only to
depart from the Lord (1:6*a*). Whether they were seduced by
their own lusts or embraced evil for the sake of personal gain is
not known. What is clear is that knowing God's attitude
toward those practices (see 2 Kings 17:12-13, 16), they nevertheless willfully and deliberately engaged in them. They may
have thought they could indulge in a form of religious syncretism, but they were wrong: when it comes to the worship of
the "Lord of glory," God demands purity of heart and ad-
herence to His revealed will.

The prophet described the second group not as persons who
had in any way sought to worship God or to inquire of Him,
not as persons who were openly opposed to God (1:6*b*). Instead, Zephaniah depicted them as being indifferent to His
claims. As with many today, they probably took pride in their
self-righteousness and did not see the need to acknowledge
God in their lives. They did not want to appear entirely pagan,
however, and so in contrast to those who made a habit of
swearing in the name of *Yahweh,* they took oaths by Milcom,
god of the Ammonites.

Whereas the Hebrews living in Zephaniah's time may have
thought that their attempts at religious syncretism had been
successful, the Lord saw things differently. Whatever their
motive may have been for their different observances and prac-

11. F. A. Tatford, *Zephaniah: Prophet of Royal Blood,* vol. 3 of *The Minor
Prophets* (Minneapolis: Klock and Klock, 1983), p. 21.

tices, the Lord Himself formally charged them for failing to seek after Him or to bring their petitions before Him. Having deliberately forsaken the God of their fathers, they had become apostate. As Theodore Laetsch points out, "[they were] perfectly satisfied to go through life without giving God and His will and word any consideration." He then concludes, "All these various forms of idolatry are mortal sins."[12]

When the abiding principles of the verses are considered, it is clear that Zephaniah's message is as timely today as when it was first uttered. On the one hand, he showed the fallacy of religious syncretism. Men today are no more successful in their attempts to draw together certain basic beliefs than the people of Judah were in the time of Zephaniah. Then, as now, ecumenical strategies were abhorrent to the Lord and did not honor Him or His Word.

On the other hand, Zephaniah demonstrated conclusively the folly of bowing down to and worshiping those ideas or practices that had become enshrined in the observances of the ungodly. It was his messsage that the desire for prosperity, human attempts to create security, and the rationalizing of human lust did not bring happiness, peace, or a sense of fulfillment.

While some may object that people today do not prostrate themselves before idols, the fact remains that they are frequently caught up on the treadmill of their desires for prosperity and security, by their attempts to rationalize their behavior. Any form of greed ("covetousness," KJV) is regarded by God as idolatry (Col. 3:5).

God's word through Zephaniah was that men needed to turn to Him, to seek Him, and to ask Him to meet their needs (1:6*b*; cf. Heb. 4:16). If men today do not do so, then they show how little they differ from those who first heard Zephaniah's warning. They demonstrate by their actions that they are characterized by similar degrees of spiritual apathy and indifference.

To the Hebrews of old, as well as to men today, God shows His amazing grace and mercy in that He for a long time

12. T. Laetsch, *The Minor Prophets* (St. Louis: Concordia, 1956), p. 356.

withholds His punishment. Such judgment, however, will not always be delayed.

b. Judgment upon Social Practices, 1:7-13

The teaching of the word of the Lord through Zephaniah in 1:7-13 was later echoed by Thomas of Celano, who in 1250 wrote his famous *"Dies irae, dies illa,"* "That day is a day of wrath," based upon this passage. The words of his hymn are still found in many hymnals. They read:

> Day of wrath, O day of mourning!
> See fulfilled the prophets' warning,
> Heaven and earth in ashes burning!

Thomas then described the "day of the Lord" as one of wrath, trouble, distress, anguish, and desolation. It would be characterized by darkness, gloominess, clouds, trumpet blasts, and the sound of alarm. Thomas's poetic portrayal of the words of Zephaniah heighten the sense of drama that lies latent in the prophet's message.

Zephaniah began the passage by instructing all who were present to "be silent before the Lord God" (1:7a, NASB). The names he used for God were *"Adonai Yahweh,"* the Sovereign LORD. In executing judgment upon the earth, God would be manifested in His sovereign majesty. He would demonstrate that He alone has the right to administer justice on the earth. For this reason, noise and clamor are to give way to silence. Before Him every mouth is to be shut, and those who will have so far offended His Majesty with seeming impunity must then endure His enmity.

When the verse is read in light of Psalm 2, it also appears as if the command to "be silent" included in it instruction to cease from all opposition to the Lord, for all such opposition will be useless.

In 1:7b, the prophet introduces another description of the day of the Lord. The definite article is not used with *yom,* "day," and must be supplied in translation. Its absence seems to underscore the fact that before the final "day of the Lord" comes there will be other occasions when He will intervene in history.

The metaphor employed in verse 7 is one involving sacrifice. "The Lord has consecrated His called ones." The imagery was taken from the Mosaic legislation regarding the different sacrificial meals apointed to Israel. In view of the fact that divine preparations had been made for the outpouring of God's wrath upon the guilty, Zephaniah described as a sacrifice the justice to be meted to the unrighteous. It would be a holy act in which God's righteousness would be vindicated. The symbolism seems to have been taken primarily from the peace offering.

In Leviticus 3:1-17 and 7:11-21, the animal to be sacrificed as a peace offering was brought to the priest. The offerer identified himself with the animal by laying his hands upon the animal's head. If the animal was accepted, then he too was accepted in it. If, however, his sacrifice was rejected, then he was rejected also. In accordance with Isaiah 34:6, Jeremiah 46:10 and Ezekiel 39:17-21, in Zephaniah 1:7 the Lord uses that kind of sacrifice as a symbol of the destruction He was about to inflict. Judah was no better than her Gentile neighbors. Accordingly, she was to be judged in the same way.

What appears strange is that in verse 7 God is described as having consecrated His invited guests ("called ones") to the "feast" (cf. Isa. 13:3). The identity of the guests is deliberately left vague. Although some have imagined they were heathen nations whom Israel hoped would be destroyed by the Lord at His appearing, that interpretation seems unlikely. Merrill F. Unger conjectures that they were the Chaldeans, who were to be the instrument to chastise Judah for her sins.[13] If he is correct, then it must be borne in mind that Habakkuk's prophecy predicted the overthrow of the Chaldeans and their judgment following the ruthless oppression of God's people. It seems preferable to leave unresolved the identity of the "guests."

The symbolism of "invited guests" adheres, however, to the teaching of the book of Leviticus, for there, the worshiper, having been brought into a right relationship with the Lord, invited guests to share the meal with him. Without pressing the symbolism too far, God shows in Zephaniah 1:7*b* that He, too, has invited "consecrated guests" to feast with Him.

As verses 8-13 are considered, it is apparent that God indicted five separate classes of people in Judah. The first were the civil leaders, namely, the "rulers" and the "sons of the king." They were responsible for dispensing justice and alleviating the oppression of the poor (cf. 1 Kings 4:2; 9:23; 20:14; Jer. 24:1; 36:12). Because Josiah himself was not named, some expositors have imagined a discrepancy in the text. Rather than presuming upon such a possibility, it is preferable to conclude that Zephaniah anticipated Josiah's early death and that his prophecy referred to a later period when the power of his sons would be considerably weakened. Judah and Jerusalem would then be governed principally by the elders, who of course would discuss matters of state with the king. Such a view is in accord with 2 Kings 22:14-20; 23:30-37. Josiah's sons were to suffer in the judgment that would come upon Judah, because they had declined to walk in the ways of their father. They had become guilty of the sins and excesses that had characterized those kings of the past who, unlike David, "did not walk in the way of the Lord" (Zeph. 1:6; contrast Jehoshaphat, 2 Chron. 17:3, with Jehoram, 2 Chron. 21:12; and Ahaz, 2 Chron. 28:2, with Josiah, 2 Chron. 34:2).

A second group to come under sentence were those who had arrayed themselves in "foreign apparel" (cf. Num. 15:38; Deut. 22:11, 12). While some writers have felt that this reference applied to courtiers who dressed in expensive attire imported from countries such as Assyria, several thoughts may be discerned to underlie the charge brought against them by the Lord. The imitation of pagan nations for the sake of being "fashionable" was seen by God as an indication of the acceptance on the part of His people of the manners and customs of those who would soon pass into oblivion. In their dress, He saw also a violation of His command to His people to be separate from those about them. The style of one's dress was a subtle indication of the values of the wearer. In Judah, wearing what was fashionable linked the wearer with the life-style of the people from whose country his clothing was acquired.[14] In assessing the sincerity of His people, God could see that while they may have worshiped Him with their lips, their hearts were far from Him.[15]

A third group to be singled out by God were the persons who leaped "over the threshold" (1:9a).

At first this expression is bewildering. What can it possibly mean? As one traces the word *threshold* through Scripture, it is evident that the word referred to the threshold of a temple or sacred building (1 Sam. 5:4, 5; Ezek. 9:3; 10:4; 46:2; 47:1). It was never used of a private dwelling. It would seem, therefore, that the practice mentioned in Zephaniah involved some form of pagan superstitution.

In antiquity, the threshold was judged to be the abode of demons. As a consequence, it was a place of particular danger. In Roman times (and even in our own), such a belief found expression in the practice of carrying a bride across the threshold into her new home. It was believed that if she should stumble while crossing the threshold, that would be a bad omen and blight the marriage in any number of ways.

The use of the word *threshold* in Scripture to refer to the entrance to a temple or other building devoted to sacred purposes can be seen in 1 Samuel 5, which tells of the Philistine god Dagon falling across the threshold. As a consequence, no one entering the temple in Ashdod would step on the threshold (1 Sam. 5:5). In the course of time, the reason for the practice was undoubtedly forgotten. The practice continued, however, and the Lord held His people guilty for applying the heathen rite to their religious observances.

Closely associated with that form of pagan superstition were those who filled "the house of their masters' (i.e., the temple of their gods) with violence and deceit" (1:9b). Some have held that in 1:9b the Lord was condemning the worship of pagan gods, a view reflected in the NASB translation. Others, basing their view upon Jeremiah 22:13-17, have held that the condem-

14. *Broadman Bible Commentary,* ed. Clifton J. Allen et al., rev. ed. (Nashville: Broadman, 1972), 7:279.
15. Cf. Laetsch, p. 360.

nation was of servants employed by a wealthy landlord. In order to please "their master" they had accumulated riches for him by every expedient known to man.[16] God looked upon such practices as the inevitable result of pursuing non-*Yahwistic* standards of worship and morality.

On account of their violence and cruelty, those who had engaged in oppression and deceit were to be judged. Their actions had not escaped the eye of the Lord, and in 1:10-13 He announced His intention of calling upon them to face the consequences of their deeds and described exactly how judgment would come upon them. The "day of the Lord" would be a terrifying day of reckoning for all who had offended God.

In contrast to the silence required of those about to receive sentence, the execution of God's justice would be accompanied by a loud noise and the cry of anguish (1:10-11). At the Chaldean invasion "crying from the fish gate," "wailing from the second quarter," and "a loud crash from the hills" would be heard. The fish gate was a northern gate leading into Jerusalem (cf. Neh. 3:3; 12:39), and it may have received its name because of its proximity to the fish market. The precise location of the second quarter is uncertain. Presumably it was an addition to the city and may have been the northern area enclosed by Manasseh (2 Kings 22:14; 2 Chron. 33:14). If so, then it was a newer part of the city extending west and north from the Temple area. The hills from which the loud crash was to emanate were not specified. They may have made up a distinct section of the city called "the heights," or they may simply have been some of the hills upon which Jerusalem was built.

The point made by the Lord was that when the day of reckoning came, the victorious shouts of the invaders would be coupled with their ruthless slaughter of the inhabitants of Jerusalem. That would bring about the kind of wailing, lamentation, and destruction described in the verses. Feinberg points out that verse 10 depicts the progress of the enemy until they occupied the most prominent positions in the city.[17]

Zephaniah specifically mentioned a place called the

16. *Broadman Bible Commentary,* 7:280.
17. C. L. Feinberg, *The Minor Prophets* (Chicago: Moody, 1976), p. 48.

Maktesh, "mortar." This noun is not found elsewhere in the Old Testament as a proper name. From the text it appears to refer to a portion of the city that was at the lower elevation. More than likely, therefore, the mortar was situated in the southern part of Jerusalem. Such a view fits well with the other geographic references in the passage. The attack upon Jerusalem would come from the north (the fish gate); spread to the second quarter, where the wealthy lived in their luxurious dwellings; then ascend a high section of the city; and culminate in the southern part, where traders, merchants, and money changers met to haggle over rates of exchange and the cost of their goods. All alike were to be destroyed. There is every indication that the business practices of those in the *Maktesh* were unscrupulous. As a consequence, they were no better than the Canaanites whom God had expelled in the face of the Israelites following the Exodus of His people from Egypt.

The Lord described the shrewd and crafty traders of the *Maktesh* as "those carrying silver" (1:11*b*). In the day of their calamity the wealth which they had labored so hard to accumulate would be regarded as a burdensome weight (cf. 1:18; Hab. 2:6).

In 1:10-11, as in other parts of the prophecy, the events described pertained to the destruction of Jerusalem by Nebuchadnezzar, and to the final coming of *the* "day of the Lord," specifically His judgment upon commercial Babylon (Rev. 18).

In the closing scene of the section (1:12-13), Zephaniah used human imagery to describe the thoroughness of God's judgment. No one will be allowed to escape, for the Lord will search the streets, lanes, hovels, and underground passages of Jerusalem with lamps to uncover all who are worthy of His justice. His penetrating eyes will search out the guilty wherever they have taken refuge. There will be no possibility of hiding from Him. None of the natural hideouts or artificial caves and tunnels that honeycombed the hill on which Jerusalem had been built will be able to safeguard the unrighteous from the Lord.

So graphic and accurate was Zephaniah's description of

events to come, that the fourth-century A.D. scholar and Bible translator, Jerome, in elaborating on the overthrow of Jerusalem by Nebuchadnezzar, was able to observe that "princes and priests and mighty men were dragged even out of sewers and caves and pits and tombs, in which they had hidden themselves for fear of death."

We might have imagined that after so thorough a judgment, Zephaniah would either have run out of words or else have changed the subject to the remnant. The prophet, however, was not yet through. He had not exhausted his use of metaphors to describe the condition of the people. In 1:12, using as his illustration the process of fermentation, he described the way in which his countrymen would face God's judgment. They would be thick and sluggish.

After the grapes have been squeezed, the wine is allowed to stand in a vat for a period of time so that the accumulation of sediment can sink to the bottom. The sediment is left only long enough for it to acquire sufficient strength, color, and flavor. Then the wine is strained by being poured from one vessel to another (cf. Isa. 25:6; Jer. 48:11). If the liquid were allowed to stand longer, it would become thick and syrupy, and soon would be unpalatable.

The metaphor that Zephaniah used was stronger than the word "settled" and portrayed the idea of "thickened" or "hardened"—a reference that F. A. Tatford takes to refer to the hard crust that sometimes formed on the surface of fermented wine if it was left undisturbed for a long period of time. By comparing the people of Jerusalem to the "dregs" that proverbially "settled on their lees" (cf. Jer. 48:11), he illustrated their inability to move quickly and avoid God's judgment.

It is impossible to read the verses in Zephaniah or to consider their teaching without drawing a parallel between Zephaniah's time and our own. The mood of our times, the apathy of many people toward the Lord, the obsession with riches, and the overall religious indifference intimate to us that today, as then, men have allowed a preoccupation with things to come between themselves and the Lord.

What is even more tragic today, is the attitude of heart of those who, like Judah, have "settled on their lees." They have become spiritually indifferent and say, with Judah, "The Lord will not do us good nor will He do evil" (1:12b). They attribute to God a disinterest that is actually characteristic of their own attitude toward Him.

In spite of the warnings of God's prophets prior to the time of Zephaniah, the people of Judah had persisted in their belief that God would neither bless them if they honored Him nor bring calamity upon them if they ignored the teachings of His messengers. To all, the Lord stated that He would search out the impious and impertinent and judge them for their apathy and indifference.

The fallacy of living only for this world was graphically portrayed by Zephaniah in the closing words of verse 13. People would build homes with little thought of the morrow and would plant vineyards with every expectation of reaping the rewards of their labors. Yet in fact, they would neither dwell in the houses they had erected nor drink of the wine from the vines they had cultivated. Because of their lack of spiritual sensitivity, judgment would overtake them and they would learn too late the dangers inherent in their temporal preoccupation.

2. DESCRIPTION OF JUDGMENT, 1:14-18

Lest there should be any doubt about the nature of the forthcoming judgment, in 1:14-18 Zephaniah added intensity and vivid detail to his narration of the events. In many respects, he moved in those verses away from a general summary of what God intended to do that had appeared in 1:7-13 to the specifics that would characterize the "day of the Lord." In that day all false confidences would be swept aside. There would be no place for complacency. The passage is so intense the reader can almost hear the rumblings of war in the distance.

Unger observes that in the verses mention is made of "nine significant things" about the "great day of the Lord" (1:14; cf. 30:7; Ezek. 30:3; Joel 1:15; 2:1; Mal. 4:5; Acts 2:20; Rev. 6:17).[18] He notes that the conditions described in the passage

18. Unger, 2:1927.

are so terrible the Chaldean invasion could only be a prefigure-
ment of a period of unprecedented tribulation that will one day
break forth (Dan. 12:1; Matt. 24:21). The entire paragraph,
therefore, may be seen in its larger scope as illustrating God's
judgment during the Tribulation period.

a. Its Imminence, 1:14

The Hebrew text of 1:14 is so emphatic in describing the approach of that great day that in the English translation the
word "near" ought to be given special emphasis: "*Near* [is] the
great day of the Lord. [It is] *near* and coming very quickly."
To those living in Jerusalem, however, Zephaniah's words may
have appeared empty. Under Josiah, the nation was ex-
periencing greater prosperity than it had known for many
decades. Its main enemy, Assyria, was facing a period of
political and economic decline.

Why then should God's people be overly concerned about a
priest's prediction of impending doom? Was not, therefore, a
new day about to dawn? Surely the prospects of the nation of
Israel appeared bright. All the nation had to do was keep pace
with the times.

Such self-satisfaction in the people of Israel may have been
the reason Zephaniah underscored the imminence of the coming destruction. He wanted them to heed his warnings and to
prepare their hearts in sincere repentance before the storm
clouds broke upon them in full fury. In picturing the events of
the calamitous period to come, he described the scene as if he
had witnessed it. It would be a time of fear and bloodshed.
Everything would be thrown into confusion. Seasoned war-
riors would cry out in anguish. The Lord would take severe
vengeance upon the guilty. Those who had turned a deaf ear to
God's entreaties through His prophets would not be able to
withstand His wrath. Their disillusionment, despair, and utter
helplessness would be apparent to all. Even the most powerful
of the people would succumb to fear.

b. Its Indignation, 1:15-18

In 1:15-18, Zephaniah provided the most condensed summary of the "day of the Lord" to be found in Scripture. That

day would be "the time of Jacob's trouble" (Jer. 30:5-7). The land would be laid waste (Nah. 2:10).

In describing the horrors of that day of judgment, Zephaniah marshaled his powers of description (1:15). The Hebrew text is even more impressive and awe-inspiring than an English translation. The fate awaiting Judah precluded any thought of hope or last minute deliverance. Black thunderclouds would envelope the land, and the lightening bolts of God's wrath would wreak havoc and destruction.

As Zephaniah continued his description of events to come, he spurred the imagination of his hearers with the sound of trumpet blasts heralding the approach of the enemy (cf. Amos 2:2). On a coming day, a battle cry would be heard, spurring on the invaders as they captured the "fortified cities" and the "high corner towers" (1:16, NASB). No city or person would be able to withstand their advance, for even the most inaccessible and strongly fortified tower would be unable to hold out against the onrush of the enemy on that day (1:16).

So distressing would this period be that those in the cities would "walk around like blind men" (1:17; cf. Deut. 28:29). Trouble would surround them. Anguish and fear would rob them of their strength. Zephaniah proclaimed that the reason they would experience such distress and discomfort was that they had sinned against the Lord. As a consequence, there would be no escape. Their punishment would be just. In that purging of iniquity, rich and poor would share alike the result of their departure from the Lord. Those who had trusted in their riches (1:18; cf. Ps. 49:6-9; Ezek. 7:19) would find that their earthly possessions would not buy them favor before the righteous anger of a just God.

The effects of the divine visitation would be universal. All mankind would suffer the penalty of God's outraged holiness. Just retribution would fall upon "all the earth" and the "fire of His jealousy" would make a "complete end" of all mankind (1:18). The whole earth would be consumed by the fire of God's wrath (cf. Rev. 20:9, 11; 2 Pet. 3:10-12).

Although a similar kind of complacency characterizes people today, it should be remembered that Christ's return is now much nearer than when men first believed (cf. Rom. 13:11-14). Soon opportunities for service will be forever gone. Being acquainted with the urgency of the hour, believers, therefore, should be diligent in service.

As God's spokesman, Zephaniah appealed to the people of God to repent. Though judgment could not be averted, those who turned to the Lord would be preserved.

3. PURPOSE BEHIND THE WARNING, 2:1-3

In calling upon the people of Judah to "gather" themselves together, Zephaniah used a term that quite literally meant to stoop down as though one were gathering stubble from a field after the reapers had passed by. The expression could only mean that God's people were to bow low before Him. In the next few words, Zephaniah conveyed the need for such contrition. God found His people to be no better than pagans. The word Zephaniah used for "nation" was not the usual Hebrew term, but rather was a term applied to Gentiles who did not know God (cf. Eph. 2:12). The nation was not ashamed of its sins and manifested no genuine longing for God or desire to serve Him.

Zephaniah's words were designed to have an effect. He did not try to placate the people or give them a false hope of deliverance. Instead, he referred to them as a "shameless nation" and warned them that God's decree (cf. Deut. 28:15) was about to be put into effect. If they failed to repent now, the storm of divine wrath would sweep over them "like the chaff " (NASB), and the fury of *Yahweh's* anger would be meted out to them.

Historically, of course, we know that God's people did not turn to Him. They spurned that offer of grace. A remnant, however, did seek His face and was spared (cf. Jer. 30:5-9; Joel 2:14; Amos 5:15). In 2:3 they were described as the "humble of the land" (lit. the "meek of the earth") who had done His justice. They would be "hidden" on the day of God's wrath. The Hebrew term conveyed the idea of protection, as if the person concerned were being sheltered from the weather. The expression illustrated God's grace in that He did not indiscriminately punish a people deserving of judgment without first giving those whose hearts were inclined toward Him the opportunity to repent.

In much the same way, in the last days a Jewish remnant will be preserved through the horrors of the Tribulation (Rev. 12:13-17). Even in judgment God remembers mercy.

8

I. JUDGMENT OF THE DAY OF THE LORD, 1:1—3:8 (*CONTINUED*)

C. JUDGMENT UPON THE NATIONS, 2:4-15

H. A. Ironside, in his commentary on the Minor Prophets, draws our attention to a principle that is alluded to over and over again in Scripture, namely, that while God will overlook nothing in Israel's ways that merits rebuke, He will also visit the severest judgment on all who lift their hands against them.

Having announced His judgment upon Jerusalem and Judah, God directed His prophet's attention to the surrounding nations: Philistia in the west (2:4-7), Moab and Ammon in the east (2:8-11), Ethiopia in the south (2:12), and Assyria in the north (2:13-15). He then returned to deal with His chosen people once more (3:1-7).[1]

The new section of the prophecy was closely connected with the preceding by the word $k\bar{\imath}$, "for." Judgment would purge out sinners from among the Gentiles, just as judgment on Jerusalem and Judah would purge out apostates from among God's people (Ezek. 20:37-38).[2]

1. JUDGMENT UPON PHILISTIA IN THE WEST, 2:4-7

In 2:4-7 the prophet asserted that Israel's ancient enemy, Philistia, would be the first to be judged. Destruction was forecast upon the cities of Gaza, Ashkelon, Ashdod, and Ekron. Interestingly, Gath was ommitted, possibly because it had never fully recovered from its defeat by Uzziah (2 Chron.

1. H. A. Ironside, *The Minor Prophets* (Neptune, N.J.: Loizeaux, 1976), p. 309.
2. The authenticity of almost every verse in this chapter has been questioned by one critic or another. The objections have all been answered by modern writers. For a summary, see James Orr, ed., *International Standard Bible Encyclopedia* (Grand Rapids: Eerdmans, 1929), 5:3145.

26:6) and had failed to regain its rank within the Philistine pentapolis (cf. Amos 1:6-8).

The oracle against Philistia began with the threat of judgment (*hōi,* "woe"). The land was to be left desolate. Gaza would be abandoned. Ashkelon would become a desolation. The attack upon Ashdod would be so surprising that the people would be driven out in the heat of the noonday sun. And Ekron would be uprooted.

Philistine occupation of the coastal plain dated back to the time of Abraham (c. 2000 B.C.; Gen. 21:32). Originally of Hamitic descent, the Philistines had probably come from the island of Crete (Amos 9:7). Though they seemed secure, Zephaniah intimated that the storm of adversity, which was to sweep over the entire country, would have a devastating effect upon them. Their depopulated coastlands would become pasture for sheep, and, to protect themselves from the heat of the sun, Nomadic shepherds would make themselves shelters out of caves or huts dug out of the ground. As a result of God's judgment upon them, the area that had once teemed with life would become a desolation whose only inhabitants were wandering shepherds tending their flocks of sheep. In place of the vigorous sea trade that had characterized the Philistines for centuries, the land would become the possession of the remnant of God's people (cf. 1 Sam. 30:14; Ezek. 25:16).

2. JUDGMENT UPON MOAB AND AMMON IN THE EAST, 2:8-11

Continuing to speak through His prophet, God now turned His attention to those nations on Judah's eastern border. The Moabites and Ammonites were both descendants of Abraham's nephew, Lot. When Lot had escaped with his daughters from Sodom, his daughters had feared that they would never marry or bear children of their own. Conniving together, they had made their father drunk and successively had had sexual intercourse with him. The sons born of the incestuous relationships had become the progenitors of the Moabites and Ammonites (Gen. 19:36-38). Those two nations had consistently opposed God's people. They had rejoiced at every calamity suffered by God's people (for Moab, see Num. 22:1-6; 25:1-8;

Judg. 3:12ff.; 2 Kings 3:4ff.; 2 Chron. 20:1ff.; Ezek. 25:8; and for Ammon, see Judg. 11:4-33; 1 Sam. 11:1-11; 2 Sam. 10:1-14; 2 Chron. 20:1ff.; Neh. 2:10, 19; 4:3-23; Jer. 40:14). As a result, the prophets frequently denounced them for their inveterate hatred of Israel and Judah (Jer. 48:1—49:6; Ezek. 25:1-11). Now, on account of their pride and arrogance (Isa. 16:6), gross immorality, idolatry (1 Kings 11:7), and sociopathic inhumanity (2 Kings 3:26-27), they were to suffer divine retribution.

It is ironic that the Moabites and Ammonites claimed that their land had been given them by their principle deity. Chemosh of the Moabites and Molech of the Ammonites (cf. Num. 21:29 and 1 Kings 11:7) have often been identified with one another.[3] Even though they had certain ritualistic obser- vances in common, it is better to keep them separate. They would be powerless to protect their devotees in the day of God's anger.

It is important to observe that God had taken note of the haughtiness and oppression of Moab and Ammon, and of their inhumanity toward persistent opposition to His people (2:8). In opposing the Hebrews they had unwittingly reviled and vaunted themselves against the Lord. Their day of reckoning had at last come. Their judgment was to be utter and complete.

Zephaniah indulged in historical reflection as well as eschatological prediction as he described what was about to take place. The two nations, having come into being when Lot escaped the judgment that fell upon Sodom and Gomorrah, were now to share the fate of the cities. Their punishment would be as permanent as it would be irrevocable. No hope was given them, and no offer of clemency was extended to those who might repent. Instead, their fate was sealed with an oath (2:9).

Their land, which for centuries had been noted for its fertil- ity, would become desolate waste. Coarse nettles and salt pits would destroy its fertility. Accordingly, it would become a land of permanent desolation and would serve as a continuous

---

3. See "Gods, False," *Unger's Bible Dictionary,* ed. M. F. Unger, 3d ed. (Chicago: Moody, 1966), pp. 414-16.

reminder of the folly of pride and of the end result of those who magnify themselves against the Lord and the people whom He has chosen (2:10).

In pondering Zephaniah's prophecy, what Henry Wadsworth Longfellow had to say comes to mind:

> The mills of God grind slowly,
> Yet they grind exceeding small;
> Though with patience He stands waiting,
> With exactness grinds He all.

All persons need to be constantly reminded that God weighs a man's actions and discerns the thoughts and intents of his heart. No one can escape the consequences of his deeds. The judgment of God upon Moab and Ammon was just. Their arrogance and inhumanity had caused them unwittingly to take sides against the Lord. As such, they shared the fate reserved for all who opposed Him. Evildoers, together with the "gods" they had chosen to serve, were to be laid waste and destroyed (2:11).

3. JUDGMENT UPON ETHIOPIA IN THE SOUTH, 2:12

With a sudden shift of focus, the Lord now directed the attention of His prophet to a nation lying to the south of Judah. That nation was "the land of Ethiopia" (cf. Isa. 20:4; Ezek. 30:4-9). The reference seems to have been to the Cushites who inhabited the land south and southwest of Egypt. They were the descendants of Cush, the son of Ham (Gen. 10:6), and they controlled the area now known as eastern Sudan, Ethiopia, Somalia, and Eritrea. Ethiopia is also mentioned in 3:10, where the reference may be to the White and Blue Nile Rivers and their many tributaries (cf. Isa. 18:1).

The Ethiopians ruled Egypt from 720 to 654 B.C., and that has led some commentators to believe that it was Egypt rather than Ethiopia that Zephaniah had in view. The dating of Josiah's reign and Zephaniah's prophecy, of course, is important in determining the people who were addressed. The evidence favors Ethiopia.

Ethiopia had been a great nation. At times she had threatened the well-being of Judah (cf. 2 Kings 19:9; 2 Chron. 14:9-13; see also Isa. 37:9). The Ethiopians had been decisively defeated by Esarhaddon prior to 669 B.C. Now further destruction was predicted.

God's sentence against Ethiopia was to be executed by the sword. The country was to be ravaged by war. The descendants of Cush would perish at the hands of invaders whom the Lord would send against them. They would learn too late that the Lord is sovereign over the whole earth and holds the destiny of each individual and nation in His hand. No matter how powerful they may have been, their deeds would be evaluated in light of their treatment of His chosen people (cf. Matt. 25:31-46).

4. JUDGMENT UPON ASSYRIA IN THE NORTH, 2:13-15

As Zephaniah turned his attention from the dismal specter of the destruction of the territories lying to the south of Judah, his gaze was directed northward. That was the direction from which trouble invariably came to those living in Israel and Judah. Syria lay to the north, and Assyria and Babylonia took advantage of the well-watered area of the Tigris-Euphrates River valley north of Israel whenever they chose to attack God's people, rather than march their armies across the desert.

Now, however, it was Assyria that came within the scope of God's decree. The nation had dominated events in the ancient Near East from the time of Ashurnasirpal II (883 B.C.) to the time of Zephaniah's prophecy. Although that great colossus had begun to totter, its downfall was not as apparent to those living in Judah as it is today in hindsight.

Through Zephaniah, the Lord declared that He was about to stretch out His hand against Assyria. Although those in Judah did not know it yet, Media and Babylonia would shortly join forces and attack Assyria. Although not immediately successful, the invaders would march against Assyria, and Nineveh, one of the oldest cities in the world (Gen. 10:11), would succumb soon after. Judgment upon the Assyrians would be decisive. The people, known for their rapacious cruelty (Nah. 3:1), would suffer the consequences of their sins.

Their city would become a complete desolation.

The method God chose to bring about the destruction of the Assyrians was most interesting. Nineveh was deemed to be an impregnable city, for its strength was impressive. It had been embellished more than any other city since the dawn of civilization. Inside its walls were parks, botanical gardens, and a zoo. The king boasted of a library of more than seventeen thousand clay tablets. Palaces had been built, and sculptured walls depicted the exploits of the various kings. Conduits brought fresh water from springs thirty miles away, and an aqueduct had been constructed to control the flooding of one of the nearby rivers. To further make Nineveh impervious to attack, the walls around the city had been enlarged and strengthened.

Xenophon, the ancient Greek historian, stated that those walls stood one hundred feet high and were fifty feet thick. They were surrounded by a moat one hundred fifty feet wide, and the city was further protected by twelve hundred towers. As a result, the Ninevites thought they could withstand an attack indefinitely.

In spite of its grandeur and power, Nineveh was destined to be swept away. The first century (B.C.) historian Diodorus Siculus refers to a legend that stated that the city would not be taken until the river became its enemy (cf. Nah. 1:8; 2:6; 3:13, 15). History records that when the Medes and Babylonians attacked Nineveh, there was a sudden rise in the level of the Tigris River. Water began to soften the sun-dried bricks. A section of the wall collapsed, causing a breach in the once-proud city's defenses. It was soon overrun and destroyed.

So complete was Nineveh's overthrow that for centuries it became the habitat of wild animals. In the course of time, grass grew over the ruins, and when Alexander the Great marched his armies up the Tigris-Euphrates Valley, Nineveh had been so completely covered that Alexander and his army were unaware that beneath their feet lay the mighty city of Nimrod (Gen. 10:8-11).

The exactness with which God's Word has been fulfilled in ages past gives valuable clues as to how it will be fulfilled in the future. God's judgments are precise. His knowledge is absolute. His will is all-powerful. The pride of Nineveh was abased. As soon as the cup of her iniquity was full, she perished. The exactness with which this prophecy was fulfilled provides a startling preview of the overthrow of nations and kingdoms at the end times. Such contemplation should fill each God-fearing believer with reverential awe. All that the Lord has spoken of, will assuredly come to pass. And it will happen exactly as He said it would.

D. JUDGMENT UPON JERUSALEM, 3:1-7

After proclaiming God's judgment upon the nations surrounding Judah, the prophet returned to his initial theme (1:4—2:3). He focused attention upon the capital city and, speaking on behalf of the Lord, made one final appeal. Having demonstrated what He was about to do to the nations surrounding Judah, God demonstrated His grace toward His people by warning them of impending judgment. In doing so, He appealed to them to repent.

1. SUMMARY OF THE CAUSE OF JUDGMENT, 3:1-2

In the concluding section of the passage, Jerusalem was depicted as being no better than her pagan neighbors. She had sunk so low that she was no longer regarded as a "city of peace," but was instead described as a city given over to oppression. It was no wonder, therefore, that Zephaniah began with a strong, assertive statement, "Woe to her."

Faithfulness to the Lord on the part of those in Jerusalem would have resulted in obedience to the law. Obedience would have manifested itself in the care of the poor and the needy. Instead, those living in Jerusalem were rebellious and spiritually filthy. Their disobedience to the revealed will of God would result in chastisement.

The participle, *morah,* "rebelling," translated "rebellious" in the NASB, carried with it the connotation of defiance. When paired with the other participle, *g'l,* "defiling," translated "defiled" in the NASB, it conveyed the idea of something irrevocably stained. Ironically, *g'l* is from the same root as the word found in the book of Ruth, *go'el,* used to describe the kinsman-redeemer. The tragedy thus brought forward in the passage was that the very people God had redeemed had rebelled against Him, thereby incurring His judgment. They had persisted in their folly to the point of becoming completely defiled.

With rebellion against the Lord and continued evil staining the lives and conduct of the people, it was no wonder that the city had become characterized by oppression (from *yānă*, "to do wrong," translated "tyrannical" in the NASB). In oppressing one another, those in Jerusalem demonstrated the true nature of immorality. Immorality arises whenever people are treated like things and things are valued as if they were people; in place of sound judgment and moral equity, the rich exploit the poor, and all of the sins accompanying vice and avarice are practiced openly and without shame.

In indicting the nation, Zephaniah stated four things about the city:

- She had not listened to the word of the Lord.
- She had not received instruction through His messengers.
- She had not trusted in Him.
- She had not drawn near to Him in penitence and contrition.

From Jeremiah 22:21, it is evident that the people had refused to conform to the revealed will of God. He had spoken to them through His prophets, but the voice of correction had gone unheeded. As a consequence, social and moral degradation had followed. The inhabitants of Jerusalem had violated the reproof of conscience. They had had no desire for the discipline of the spirit. They had not seen God's hand in their chastisements (Ps. 78:22; Jer. 13:25) and had remained obstinate and unrepentant of heart.

As deplorable as the spiritual condition of Judah was, men today have no grounds for boasting that they are better. In lands long enlightened by the gospel, the same form of rejection can be seen. God's Word is not honored and its message is not heeded. Trust is placed in human leaders, and there is a general insensitivity to sin. As a consequence, few are prepared to accept the discipline of sons of God (Heb. 12:5-13). The end result is that in many communities Christians can scarcely be distinguished from their pagan neighbors. Only here and there is a godly person to be found. As with the nation of Judah, only a remnant still heed and practice the Word of the Lord. Their comfort is that the Lord is aware of their deeds and will succor them in times of adversity.

When the reader today reflects on 3:1-2 and relates those to what follows, it is clear that when moral torpor and personal apathy are combined, the way is paved for debased human leadership.

2. SPECIFIC PEOPLE TO BE JUDGED, 3:3-4

Having outlined the cause of Jerusalem's deplorable condition, Zephaniah then proceeded to point the finger at four specific leadership groups. To them had been committed the responsibility of reminding the Hebrews of their spiritual heritage. Zephaniah singled out the rulers, the judges, the prophets, and the priests. He then censured each group for its actions.

The rulers, or civic officials, had forfeited the right to lead God's people. Instead of instilling in the people respect for the righteous judgments of the law, they had inculcated fear. Their greed and avarice had led them to seek power and to abuse the privileges and responsibilities of their office. Zephaniah likened them to roaring lions ready to pounce upon any unsuspecting victim (cf. Prov. 28:15; Ezek. 22:27; Amos 3:4; Mic. 2:2).

The magistrates, or judges, had aided and abetted the civil rulers. To them had been committed the responsibility of protecting the poor and the innocent and of punishing the guilty. Zephaniah likened them to "wolves at evening" who were ravenous and fierce, merciless and cruel. He described their hunger as being so insatiable that they would devour anything and everything they could find, leaving nothing remaining (cf. Amos 2:6-8).

The prophets were to reveal the word of the Lord to the people and warning them of the consequences of disobedience. Instead of fulfilling their appointed role, the prophets had engaged in the very vices they should have condemned. As a consequence, they had become proud (*rohāzîm*, "empty, without substance, fickle," translated "reckless" in the NASB) and irresponsible (cf. Jer. 6:13-14; Mic. 2:11; 3:5). They were filled with deceit and subverted the word of the Lord to serve their own evil ends.

The fourth group to have their sins and vices exposed to public view were the priests. Purity was required of them as priests. In Zephaniah's time, however, they had profaned the holy place (cf. Jer. 7:9-11). They had despised God's law. They were the "theological liberals" of their day. In effect, they had rewritten the ritual of God's service, redefining what He required, and, instead of safeguarding and teaching the truth (Lev. 10:11; Deut. 31:9-13), had sought only to secure for themselves positions of importance, so that they could satisfy their own carnal desires. Not surprisingly, the prophet denounced them as men of treachery, who had been faithless in the discharging of their duties and who had exploited sacred office for the sake of personal gain (cf. Jer. 27:9-11; 28:1-17; 29:21-23). As Laetsch scathingly points out, "They manipulated the law of God chiefly for the purpose of filling their [own] purses."[4]

When leaders have become utterly corrupt, it is imperative that a suitable standard of righteousness be found. While the character of one's leaders may inevitably be reflected in the lives of those who are led, Zephaniah shows that God had not left Himself without witness in the city.

3. STANDARD OF RIGHTEOUSNESS TO BE UPHELD, 3:5

In contrast to the fourfold description of degradation given in 3:3-4, in 3:5 the prophet brought to the fore an example of God's unchanging righteousness: "*Yahweh* is righteous." Zephaniah stated emphatically, "Every morning He brings His justice to light; He does not fail" (NASB).

Centuries earlier, when the sons of Israel had marched

4. T. Laetsch, *The Minor Prophets* (St. Louis: Concordia, 1956), p. 375.

through the desert, God's presence had been evident in their midst by a pillar of cloud during the day and a pillar of fire at night. When the Shekinah glory, a reminder of God's character and holiness, filled Solomon's Temple, that same phenomenon occurred. A pillar of cloud was to be seen over it by day and a pillar of fire at night.[5] Every morning God's people could see the evidence of His presence in their midst. It brought to mind His holiness. Yet though He set them an example of righteousness (Mic. 3:11), they were forgetful of Him. They knew from observation and history that He would do no iniquity (cf. Isa. 9:12, 17, 21), but neither His teaching nor His suzerainty was sufficient to turn them from their sins.

Each morning He would unfailingly remind them of His presence, yet that did not prevent them from perverting justice, oppressing the poor, and performing without shame those acts that had brought down judgment upon Israel and would bring down judgment upon Judah. Jeremiah, who prophesied at about the same time as Zephaniah (cf. Jer. 6:15), stated that there was no sign of contrition among the people. They were oblivious to the holiness of God. Instead of concentrating on the development of their Godward relationship, they gave themselves over to greed, oppression, and wrong-doing of every sort.

4. STANCE OF THE PEOPLE TOWARD THE WARNING, 3:6-7

It is ironic, but those who have so hardened their hearts against the Lord neglect His reproof and become obsessed with their own self-interest. They find it difficult, if not impossible, to think that any form of judgment will overtake them.

In the case of Judah and Jerusalem, God had given the people examples of His justice. Zephaniah summarized what the Lord had done. In His manner of dealing with the surrounding nations He had provided His people with one instance after another of His righteousness and justice. All His people needed to do was recall the facts of history or gaze in awe at the ruins of some of the nations who had been overthrown. Such nations

5. Cf. C. J. Barber, "Restoring God's Image in Man," *Theological Student's Fellowship Bulletin* 71 (Spring 1975): 22-24.

had been decimated. Strongly fortified corner towers lay in ruins. The streets of metropolitan areas were deserted. No one was to be seen anywhere. The picture drawn for Judah's benefit was one of utter destruction. God had made a complete end of those who opposed Him.

Knowing, therefore, the might and power of God, it would have been expected of Jerusalem and Judah to bow in reverential awe before Him. They should have been quick to respond to His discipline and to receive instruction from Him, and thus escape being cut off like the rest (cf. Jer. 7:6-7).

Jerusalem, however, ignored God's gracious warning (3:7*c*).

E. JUDGMENT UPON ALL NATIONS, 3:8

Because God's words through His prophet had both a near and a far view, it is appropriate to conclude the discussion of the section with a consideration of 3:8. The prophet had pronounced judgment upon Jerusalem, and now looked to a future time when God would assemble all nations together and pour out His indignation upon them so that He might make an utter end of them all.

Those who are exhorted to "wait for Me" (NASB) are in all probability the godly remnant. They will see the Lord's enemies gathering themselves together for battle and will witness the outpouring of His indignation and wrath upon them. As Tatford points out, God's intolerance of sin will be evidenced by the unmitigated punishment that will be meted out to those who dare to oppose His will.[6]

The language of the verse clearly anticipates the judgment that will immediately precede the inauguration of Christ's millennial Kingdom (cf. Ps. 2). Although God's ways in judgment have been made clear throughout history, the grand climax of His program and the events of Armageddon will one day occur (3:8; cf. Rev. 16:13-16).

So it is that in spite of the opposition of man, spiritual apathy, and general inertia God will demonstrate His righteousness in the judgment.

6. F. A. Tatford, *The Minor Prophets* (Minneapolis: Klock and Klock, 1983), 1:62.

9

II. SALVATION OF THE DAY OF THE LORD, 3:9-20

Both the Old and New Testament are replete with promises about Christ's second coming. According to one authority, there are 1,845 references to Christ's rule on earth in the Old Testament, and a total of seventeen Old Testament books give prominence to the event. Of the 216 chapters in the New Testament, there are 318 references to the second coming, and it is mentioned in twenty-three of the twenty-seven books. (The four books that do not record Christ's second advent are the three single-chapter letters written to private individuals and the book of Galatians.) Something of the importance of Christ's return to set up His Kingdom may be gleaned from the fact that for every prophecy relating to His first coming, there are eight treating His second coming.

With all of the space given the event in the Bible, one might conclude that the circumstances surrounding the return of the Lord Jesus to the earth would be well known. Such is not the case. Writers from all walks of life either predict or imply that life in the future will continue in much the same way as it does at present. To those who hold such views, the writing of Zephaniah is, therefore, an enigma. To those who believe, however, Zephaniah's prophecy serves the purpose for which it was intended (1 John 3:3).

A. CONVERSION OF THE NATIONS, 3:9

As the reader connects 3:9 with the verse that precedes it, he realizes that God encouraged the people of Zephaniah's day to wait for Him because He would soon arise to judge His (and their) enemies. The Lord made clear that in executing judgment, He would gather the nations together and pour out His indignation upon them. They would feel His burning anger and realize too late His intolerance of sin. Unmitigated punishment would result from His wrath, and the whole earth would be consumed by the fire of His zeal. Divine vengeance upon sin would be exacted fully from the inhabitants of the earth.

It is difficult to argue that the language employed by God's prophet anticipates anything other than the final judgment of the earth. Earlier, partial fulfillments of the prophecy will only pave the way for the cataclysmic events of the Tribulation period.

Following the judgment of the nations at the end of the Tribulation (Matt. 25:31-46), there will be established the millennial reign of Christ. His rule will be over a redeemed people made up of both Jews and Gentiles. It is at that time that He will return (*hpk,* "to turn back, to change") to the people a pure language (*sāpâ,* "lip, speech, mouth, language"). The statement in Zephaniah 3:9 of what is yet to happen, while oblique, may refer to a coming reversal of the confusion of languages with which God punished mankind at the tower of Babel (Gen. 11:1, 6-7, 9).

Tatford has pointed out that the reference to "purified lips" (NASB) expresses the inward thoughts of those whose lives are affected by change. In Scripture, the character of one's thoughts (*i.e.,* the thoughts of one's heart) is figuratively imputed to the lips. As a consequence, in passages such as Psalm 16:4 and Hosea 2:17, those who invoke the names of idols are deemed to have "unclean lips," having become defiled as a result of taking the names of false gods "upon their lips."[1]

It has been conjectured, and perhaps with justification, that Hebrew will be the one universal language spoken during the Kingdom age (cf. Zech. 14:9). This should not appear surprising because Israel will be the chief among the nations during the Millennium (cf. Isa. 2:2-3; Zech. 8:20-23). Such unity of language anticipates the outpouring of the Holy Spirit prophesied by Joel (Joel 2:28-32) and may well facilitate the spread of the knowledge of the Lord as predicted by Habakkuk (Hab. 2:14).

1. F. A. Tatford, *Zephaniah: Prophet of Royal Blood,* vol. 3 of *The Minor Prophets* (Minneapolis: Klock and Klock, 1983), p. 62.

In contrast to Israel's past, the future worship of God's people will be characterized by purity (Zeph. 3:9*a*). They will call upon the name of the Lord and serve Him with one consent (3:9*b*; Hebrew text and NASB, "shoulder to shoulder," a metaphor used to describe unity, harmony, or perfect accord). The wicked will have been purged out and a people united in spirit will enter His millennial Kingdom. Oneness of heart and purity of purpose will characterize their lives. The Lord will be served by His people in a manner fitting the glories of His Person and His works on behalf of His people.

In pondering the blessings that are to come upon "the people" (3:9*a*), the prophet was led to expound more fully upon Israel's place among the nations of the earth. In 3:9 he described their regathering from the lands into which they will have been dispersed during the Tribulation period. In the remaining verses of the book (3:10-20) he amplified that description.

B. RESTORATION OF ISRAEL, 3:10-20

1. REGATHERING OF ISRAEL, 3:10

In accordance with His promises, the Lord will bring His worshipers back to Israel from the lands of their dispersion (cf. Isa. 11: 11-16; Ezek. 37:15-28). In the text, Zephaniah described those lands as being "beyond the rivers of Ethiopia" (NASB). The reference was undoubtedly to the region of the Blue and White Nile Rivers south of Aswan, the territory known today as Eastern Sudan, Ethiopia, Somalia, and Eritrea (Isa. 18:1; Zeph. 2:12). From those regions God's "worshipers" (*lit.* suppliants, or "burners of incense") will bring Him offerings (*minchah,* "meal offerings," cf. Lev. 2). Those offerings will indicate their recognition of the perfection of His character and work, and will have the effect of restoring the people to God's favor and preparing them for His blessing.

2. REDEMPTION OF ISRAEL, 3:11-13
a. Conversion of the Remnant, 3:11-13*a*

"In that day," at the very beginning of the millennial era, the remnant of the people who have been gathered together from the farthest corners of the earth will "look upon" Him whom they, in the person of their leaders, "have pierced; and they will mourn for Him, as one mourns for an only son, and they will weep bitterly over Him like the bitter weeping over a first-born" (Zech. 12:10, NASB; see the context of Zech. 12:10—13:1). Their contrition will lead to their forgiveness. Israel will no longer have any cause to be ashamed on account of its rebellion against the Lord, or its pride, arrogance and self-exhaltation. Those attitudes, which at one time characterized the sons of Israel, will have been removed from their midst (cf. Isa. 11:9). The remnant regathered to the land will not be ashamed before the Lord (Isa. 45:17; 54:4; Joel 2:26-27), but will exhibit true piety in its worshipful attitude toward Him.

Of course, there are those who have ridiculed the words of the prophet. It should be noted, however, that even George Adam Smith, who so frequently aligns himself with those who take issue with the plain teaching of Scripture, in this instance states categorically that a thorough purgation, resulting in the removal of the wicked (with the sparing of the honest and the meek), will characterize Messiah's reign. Faith, in its simplest form of trust in a righteous God, and character, in its basal elements of meekness and truth, will alone survive the judgment.[2]

Zephaniah continued by pointing out that those restored to the land will no longer commit iniquity or practice deceit. Their pride and arrogance will have been removed, and they will have become a humble and lowly people who take refuge in the name of the Lord. Their moral and spiritual integrity will be evident. No longer will oppression, lies, and deception characterize their actions. They will be guileless. All forms of perversity and wickedness, including idolatry, will be removed from them. The "fountain" that Zechariah saw as being "opened for the house of David and for the inhabitants of Jerusalem" will have washed away all of their sin and impurity (Zech. 13:1, NASB).

---

2. G. A. Smith, *The Book of the Twelve Minor Prophets* (New York: Harper and Brothers, 1928), 2:70-71.

b. Restoration of the Remnant, 3:13*b*

Peace and prosperity will accompany their return to the Lord. Israel will enjoy the tranquility and security foretold in type and metaphor by the prophets (cf. Ps. 80:4-19; Mic. 4:4). To that picture Zephaniah added his own description of Israel's future state. Employing the figure of a shepherd with his sheep, Zephaniah stated that Israel "shall feed and lie down" (NASB) secure in the watchful care of the Good Shepherd. The people will have no fear of being disturbed, for no one will make them afraid.

In the picture of Israel's millennial blessing, given in 3:13*b*, the prophet prepared the way for the verses which followed, in which he amplified and applied the benefits of Messiah's reign. Unger sees a sevenfold description of the millennial Kingdom in the verses:

- The millennial kingdom will be an era of supreme and exhilarating joy, 3:14;

- The millennial kingdom will be an era when the Lord's judgments against Israel have been removed, 3:15*a*;

- The millennial kingdom will be favored with the personal presence of the Lord, 3:15*b*;

- The millennial kingdom will be a time when Israel will not experience evil or fear, 3:15*c*-17*a*;

- The millennial kingdom will be a time when the Lord will rejoice over Israel as the special object of His love, 3:17*b*;

- The millennial kingdom will represent the gathering together of the saved remnant, 3:18;

- The millennial kingdom will be preceded by the Lord's judgment of Israel's oppressors and the exhaltation of the saved remnant, 3:19-20.[3]

3. M. F. Unger, *Unger's Commentary on the Old Testament* (Chicago: Moody, 1981), 2:1939-40.

3. RULER OVER ISRAEL, 3:14-17

a. Rejoicing of the People, 3:14-15a

In exaltation over all that the Lord has done for His people, the "daughter of Zion" (NASB; a poetic description of the people of Jerusalem) will shout in triumph and be jubilant of heart because the Lord will have taken away all that had previously hindered her from receiving His blessing.[4]

The causes of the Israelites' praise will, of course, be many. In the first place, the Lord will have removed (*pinnâ*, "cleared away") His judgments from them. He will also have removed their enemies. Nothing now will hinder their enjoyment of the benefits of the reign of the King in their midst (Ps. 2; Zech. 6:13).

b. Reign of the King, 3:15b

The Lord, as the King of Israel, will be central in His people's lives and worship (cf. Ezek. 37:26-28; 48:35), and He will rule over all the nations of the earth (Isa. 2:2-3). His presence will guarantee Israel's security (cf. Ps., 46:1-11), and the nation will no longer need to fear opposition from the nations surrounding it.

Zephaniah began verse 16 with the familiar words "in that day." The prophet thus brought before the mind of the reader the assurance that those in Jerusalem would not experience fear. Fear derives its strength from two important elements, namely, almightiness (the power attributed to a person, place, or thing to take away one's ability to function autonomously) and impendency (the power to do one harm). As those in Jerusalem gained confidence in the good will of their King toward them, they would encourage one another with the words, "Do not be afraid, . . . do not let your hands fall" limply by your sides as though you were too faint to carry on (3:16, NASB). In 3:17 Zephaniah gave the explanation for those words of assurance:

> The Lord your God is in your midst,
> A victorious warrior.

4. E. B. Pusey, *The Minor Prophets* (Grand Rapids: Baker, 1953), 2:288.

> He will exult over you with joy,
> He will be quiet in His love,
> He will rejoice over you with shouts of joy.

Zephaniah described the Lord as Israel's mighty *gibbŏr*, "valiant warrior," *yŏshĭā,* "who saves," or "who is victorious." The picture the prophet brought before the reader's mind was of Boaz (*'ĭsh gibbŏr ḥayil*, "mighty man of valor"), who redeemed Ruth from poverty and distress. In fulfilling the role of a kinsman-redeemer, he took her as his bride and rejoiced over her. She, on her part, entered into the "rest" of his love.[5]

The picture presented by Zephaniah was essentially the same. The prophet wrote of a coming day when the Lord would redeem His people, reinstate them in the land, and rejoice over them. As Keil so aptly points out, Zephaniah used a daring anthropomorphism to denote a love deeply felt and absorbed in its object with thoughtfulness and admiration.[6]

4. REWARD OF ISRAEL, 3:18-20

In addition to rejoicing over His people as a bridegroom rejoices over his bride, the Lord would also gather to His side those who had been oppressed or who had been scattered among the nations. Their time of mourning would be over. Their separation would be at an end. Their shame would be gone. The Lord would deal with their oppressors and would champion the cause of the lame and gather the outcasts. He would turn their former humiliation into praise, and Israel, who had formerly been despised, would be exalted to headship over the nations (cf. Deut. 28:13).

In 3:20 Zephaniah reaffirmed what he had stated. The repetition provided a fitting conclusion to the prophecy. Unger amplifies the statement in Zephaniah. " 'Incredible as all that may seem,' the Lord told Israel, 'it will be fulfilled before your

---

5. C. J. Barber, *Ruth: An Expositional Commentary* (Chicago: Moody, 1983), pp. 111-21.
6. C. F. Keil, "Zephaniah," *Bible Commentary on the Old Testament: The Minor Prophets* (Grand Rapids: Eerdmans, n.d.), 2:161.

very eyes.' "[7] It will become a delightful reality. Israel's restoration during the Millennium to renown and blessing will constitute the fullfillment of the promise God made to Abraham (Gen. 12:1-3) and will take place exactly as Zephaniah predicted.

7. Unger, 2:1940-41.

SELECTED BIBLIOGRAPHY

Anderson, J. N. D. *God's Law and God's Love.* London: Collins, 1980.

Albright, W. F. "The Psalm of Habakkuk," In *Studies in Old Testament Prophecy Presented to T. H. Robinson.* Edited by H. H. Rowley. Edinburgh: T. and T. Clark, 1950.

Archer, G. L. *Survey of Old Testament Introduction.* Chicago: Moody, 1974.

Barber, C. J. "Restoring God's Image in Man." *Theological Student's Fellowship Bulletin* 71 (Spring 1975): 22-24.

Bowker, J. *Problems of Suffering in the Religions of the World.* Cambridge: Cambridge U., 1970.

Brightman, E. S. *The Problem of God.* New York: Abingdon, 1930.

Childs, B. S. *Introduction to the Old Testament as Scripture.* Philadelphia: Fortress, 1979.

Davidson, A. B. *The Books of Nahum, Habakkuk and Zephaniah.* Cambridge Bible for Schools and Colleges. Cambridge: Cambridge U., 1905.

Driver, S. R. *The Minor Prophets.* The Century Bible. Edinburgh: T. C. and E. C. Black, 1906.

Feinberg, C. L. *The Minor Prophets.* Chicago: Moody, 1976.

Gaebelein, F. E. *Four Minor Prophets.* Chicago: Moody, 1970.

Harrison, R. K. *Introduction to the Old Testament.* Grand Rapids: Eerdmans, 1969.

Hyatt, J. P. "The Date and Background of Zephaniah," *Journal of Near Eastern Studies* 7 (1948): 25-29.

Keil, C. F. *Bible Commentary on the Old Testament: The Minor Prophets* 2 vols. Grand Rapids: Eerdmans, n.d.

Laetsch, T. *The Minor Prophets.* St. Louis: Concordia, 1956.

Luther, M. *Lectures on the Minor Prophets.* Vol. 19 of *Luther's Works.* Edited by H. C. Oswald. St. Louis: Concordia, 1974.

McClain, A. J. *The Greatness of the Kingdom.* Chicago: Moody, 1959.

Pritchard, J. B., ed. *Ancient Near Eastern Texts Relating to the Old Testament.* 2d ed. Princeton: Princeton U., 1955.

Pusey, E. B. *The Minor Prophets.* 2 vols. Grand Rapids: Baker, 1953.

Rawlinson, G. *Five Great Monarchies of the Ancient Eastern World.* 3 vols. London: J. Murray, 1871.

Smith, G. A. *The Book of the Twelve Minor Prophets.* New York: Harper and Brothers, 1928.

Tatford, F. A. *The Minor Prophets.* 3 vols. Minneapolis: Klock and Klock, 1983.

Williams, D. L. "The Date of Zephaniah," *Journal of Biblical Literature* 82 (1983): 77-88.

Moody Press, a ministry of the Moody Bible Institute, is designed for education, evangelization, and edification. If we may assist you in knowing more about Christ and the Christian life, please write us without obligation: Moody Press, c/o MLM, Chicago, Illinois 60610.